T0157502

You Are a *Star!* **Shine!**

Shiny Burcu Unsal

"The Shiny One"

BALBOA.
PRESS

A DIVISION OF HAY HOUSE

Balboa Press books may be ordered through
booksellers or by contacting:

Balboa Press
A Division of Hay House
1663 Liberty Drive
Bloomington, IN 47403
www.balboapress.com
1 (877) 407-4847

Because of the dynamic nature of the Internet, any web
addresses or links contained in this book may have changed
since publication and may no longer be valid. The views
expressed in this work are solely those of the author and do
not necessarily reflect the views of the publisher, and the
publisher hereby disclaims any responsibility for them.

The author of this book does not dispense medical advice or prescribe
the use of any technique as a form of treatment for physical, emotional,
or medical problems without the advice of a physician, either directly
or indirectly. The intent of the author is only to offer information
of a general nature to help you in your quest for emotional and
spiritual well-being. In the event you use any of the information in
this book for yourself, which is your constitutional right, the author
and the publisher assume no responsibility for your actions.

Any people depicted in stock imagery provided by Thinkstock are
models, and such images are being used for illustrative purposes only.
Certain stock imagery © Thinkstock.

Print information available on the last page.

ISBN: 978-1-5043-6144-6 (sc)
ISBN: 978-1-5043-6146-0 (hc)
ISBN: 978-1-5043-6145-3 (e)

Library of Congress Control Number: 2016911612

Balboa Press rev. date: 12/21/2016

Contents

About The Author

SHINY BURCU UNSAL

With an educational background from Harvard Business School and 15 years in communications and marketing, Shiny Burcu Unsal is the creator of Be-Live in U. She is an author, a motivational speaker, a licensed NLP trainer, an ICF-accredited life coach trainer, a top-rated course author and a lead instructor of Leadership Communication Strategies and Emotional Intelligence at UCLA Extension.

Prior to owning her mission to make people SHINE, Shiny Burcu Unsal worked at multinational advertising agencies like McCann Erickson and Ogilvy to make several Fortune 500 brands like Coca Cola, AVON, BP, Gillette, Audi, etc. shine! ⭐ And today, through her online videos, books, NLP and coaching trainings at Be-Live in U, and her Leadership and Emotional Intelligence classes she teaches at UCLA Extension, she makes thousands of personal brands shine! ⭐

Her educational background includes a BS in International Relations from METU, an Award in General Business Studies with Concentration in Marketing from UCLA Extension, an Executive Education Award in Building and Leading Customer Centric Organizations from Harvard Business School and another BS, MS and an ongoing PhD in Metaphysical Psychology from the University of Metaphysics. Shiny Burcu Unsal also had the privilege of working with the best names in the personal development and success studies such as Dr. Richard Bandler, Tony

Robbins, Les Brown, Brendon Burchard, Adam Markel, Bill Walsh and Robert Kiyosaki.

Having touched thousands of people's lives from all over the world with her passion for change and growth, Shiny Burcu Unsal has been featured on numerous international TV interviews, newspapers, magazines and radio shows. She has also spoken on several seminar and conference stages to call out the *leaders* in people and empower them to let their power shine out!

Besides all these, she is a Thought Leader at the Forbes Coaches Council *(an invitation-only community for leading business and career coaches);* the California Women's Conference's and Women Network's Executive Director for Turkey; a Strategic Partner for Success Resources, a hand-selected Ambassador for Turkey for United Nations' Olympia Awards, 12 Arts of the World and awarded as one of the 40 most influential Turkish people in US under 40.

And because she Be-Live's when we solve all the communication and behavior (mindset) problems in the world, starting with the one with ourselves, this place will be a lot more SHINIER and HAPPIER place; she literally stepped up and claimed her new American name to be "SHINY"; the one who shines and makes others shine! ⭐

Welcome

My Dear Shiny,

Welcome to your new world of cosmic STARDOM and galactic being! This cute and happy book that you are about to read is my first book! YAY! ⭐ And I am super excited that I finally got to share my voice with you!!! Yes! With you! ⭐ With the one who is supposed to read my lines right now ⭐ You are reading it because you are supposed to remind yourself that you welcome and create change as you know deep down: It's your time to shine, baby!

This is a story of transformation. This is a story of trance and re-formation of a life with love. ⭐ This is a story of finding love again. The real kind of love: Self love. This is my story, my journey of my love for me. ⭐ My love for the Shiny me. ⭐ My unconditional love for the soul I have within me. The soul that connects me to the beginning and the end. The soul that shines through me. My unconditional love for the light that shines as me.

It is not that I did not love me before. Of course I did! I always did love me! And it is a known fact indeed. ⭐ But obviously not as much as I could. I did things that hurt the living being inside of me. I did things that others said I had to, regardless of what my choice was at that given time and place. I was caged, I was prisoned and I still played the Pollyanna so that I could still smile from time to time. I played Pollyanna because it was the nature of my soul to see the beauty in everything. I did my best to cover up the holes in my soul with my first "given" and then later "comfortable" life. So I kept on going in circles, wondering what was wrong with me....

Then I woke up! I woke up to the fact that there was nothing wrong with me and I was perfectly fine being me! It was the wrong questions I asked myself that led me to second-guess myself! And thanks to NLP, I learned how to talk to myself in a far more effective way to get the best answers and best results from my Shiny self. ☆ With the power of Neuro Linguistic Programming, my own soul inside of me—my beautiful, galactic and cosmic soul—woke me up to step up to become who I really was inside! My own Shiny soul remembered that we were all part of this magnificent system of love: Our universe! Thanks to my soul's guide Prem Sola that I Be-Live my Shiny God had sent me to remind me that we are all one. And that we are all here to remember who we really are! The light workers that we are as subatomic particles of our cosmic universe; we are all here to shine and also make our galactic playmates shine! ☆

XOXO, The Shiny One

I am dedicating this book to my galactic friends who always knew that they were special; they were stardust and they were born to shine! My message to you all is:

Be-Live in U! And Let Your Power Shine Out!

XOXO, The Shiny One ☆

5 STEPS TO BECOME A GALACTIC LEADER
A STAR IS A GALACTIC LEADER.
BE-LIVE IN U & LET YOUR POWER SHINE OUT!

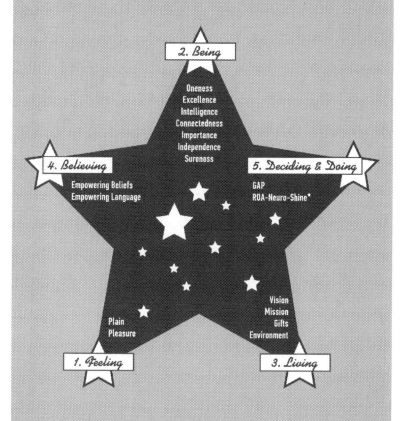

Concept of the Book

My purpose for writing this book is to show you that you are bigger than you can ever imagine!

After studying metaphysics and the laws of the universe; neuroscience and the principles of the mind for more than 10 years, I came to realize that **we are spiritual beings having a physical experience on this planet**. And we have all the power within us to make this experience an incredible one! For that, we need to understand the laws of the universe in which we live in, so that we can understand how it all works. We also need to understand how the mind works because that's the only tool we have, that can help us understand and connect even deeper with the universe so that we can create the most magnificent meanings for our lives!

An incredible experience requires a galactic level of being and a cosmic level of living. And that's exactly what you will learn from this book: how to create your cosmic life as a galactic leader!

This book is a visionary, optimistic, enlightening, empowering, energizing and celebrating philosophy about life. It teaches you how to become a galactic leader (a cosmic STAR) by combining the laws of the universe and the principles of the mind.

In order for you, as a cosmic human being to BE "**LIVE**" IN U, first you gotta BE-LIVE IN YOU! Which means you gotta Be yourself, Live Yourself and Believe in Yourself.

And here is the cosmic formula:

BE + DO = HAVE: Feeling + Being + Living + Believing + Deciding & Doing = Having the "**aliveness**."

OBJECTIVE OF THE BOOK:

- ✓ to Become a Galactic Leader
- ✓ to Live a **Shiny Happy** Cosmic Life

3 TYPES OF BEINGS:

1. Physical Beings
2. Transit Beings
3. Galactic Beings

3 TYPES OF LIVES:

1. Given Life
2. Comfortable Life
3. Cosmic Life

TEACHING METHODS / PROPOSED SELF-HELP TOOLS FOR YOU TO FIND OUT YOUR TYPE OF "BEING" AND YOUR TYPE OF "LIFE":

- ✓ 10 Cosmic Laws of the Universe For You to Be-Live in U
- ✓ 10 Galactic Rules for Galactic Leaders
- ✓ 10 Universal Principles of the Mind (NEURO LINGUISTIC PROGRAMMING) For You To Let Your Power Shine Out!

CONCEPTUAL STRATEGY:

A GALACTIC STAR-shape 5-step STRATEGY for you to BE- LIVE IN U & Let Your Cosmic Power Shine Out:

1. Feeling
2. Being
3. Living
4. Believing
5. Deciding & Doing

OFFERED LIFE TECHNOLOGIES:

- ✓ Presuppositions of NLP
- ✓ Wheel of Life Measurement
- ✓ NLP Model of Communication
  - ○ Components of Communication
  - ○ Communication Best Practices
  - ○ Chunking Technique for Deep Motivations
  - ○ Separating Identity from Behavior
  - ○ 6W+1H Contextual Intelligence

- ✓ NLP Model of Behavior
  - ○ Behavior Measurement Formula
  - ○ 10 level Behavior Positioning Chart
  - ○ Kinesiology Technique
  - ○ Human Needs Psychology
  - ○ Levels of Learning
  - ○ FEAR in Human Nature

- ✓ Conscious, Subconscious and Unconscious Minds
  - ○ Brain Waves in Human Evolution
  - ○ Interpersonal Neuro Biology & Structure of the Brain

- ○ Amygdala and its 2 F Functions

- ✓ Beliefs & Values
  - ○ Beliefs as Perception Filters
  - ○ Limiting Beliefs
  - ○ Levels of Change

<u>COMMON PROBLEMS THAT CAN BE SOLVED WITH THIS BOOK:</u>

- ✓ Victim Mentality
- ✓ Low Self-esteem
- ✓ Communication Mistakes
- ✓ Lack of Empathy
- ✓ Not Knowing What To Do in Life
- ✓ Not Knowing How To Do What You Want
- ✓ Negative Thoughts
- ✓ Unwanted Behaviors
- ✓ Blaming Others
- ✓ Lack of Confidence
- ✓ Lack of Discipline
- ✓ Lack of Motivation
- ✓ Lack of Concentration
- ✓ Procrastination
- ✓ Judging Others Too Quickly
- ✓ Trying to Change Others
- ✓ Trying to Control Things that can't be Controlled
- ✓ Negative Voices in the Head as FEARs
- ✓ Complaining About Problems
- ✓ Getting Bad Advice
- ✓ "Know it all" Attitude
- ✓ Trying to Be Right

BEST PRACTICES THAT THIS BOOK PROVIDES:

- ✓ Universal Perspective of Life
- ✓ Ability to Ask Effective Questions
- ✓ Focus Management
- ✓ Mood Management
- ✓ Clear Mission & Vision Statements
- ✓ Effective Decision Making
- ✓ Measuring Behaviors for Better Results
- ✓ Improving Self-image
- ✓ Clear and Healthy Communication
- ✓ Existential Life Design
- ✓ Re-coding Beliefs
- ✓ Self-empowerment
- ✓ Motivation
- ✓ Improving Social Skills
- ✓ Self-deprecating Humor

And eventually SHINING bright like a Diamond Galactic Leader: Like the SUN shines ⭐

5 STEPS TO BECOME A GALACTIC LEADER
A STAR IS A GALACTIC LEADER.
BE-LIVE IN U & LET YOUR POWER SHINE OUT!

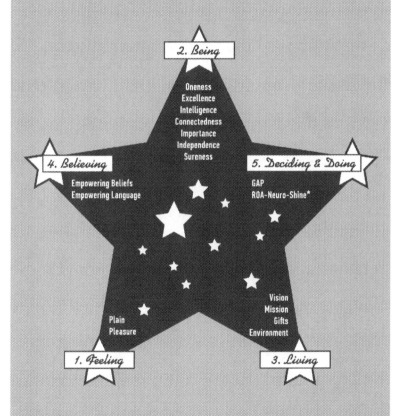

How I Let My Power Shine Out

Dear Stardust,

When you look up to the sky, has this ever happened to you? You see a star so dazzling it becomes a mesmerizing accessory to the dark night, and in that sparkling miracle, you are reminded of who you are. And have you ever noticed that this star shines at its brightest in the darkest skies, far away from the parts of the cities that are somehow a lot darker and not yet enlightened?

Well, my story began under the endless stars that shine with all their might in Anamur/Mersin, one of those not-yet-enlightened small coastal towns of Turkey. I was born on the morning of February 21, 1979, as the second and last child of a Mediterranean family who is deeply connected with love and knowledge. I loved the pleasing sea and the glittery stars that sparkled far above the dark beaches. Then those stars put a microphone in my hand (or maybe I took it on my own). For as long as I have known myself, I've been questioning myself, my life and all those wonderful, unique stars in the sky.

From the bubbly images of my childhood, I mostly remember the music, the books, and the microphone. When I look into my mind records, my files contain memories of the songs I sang during the Turkish National Sovereignty and Children's Day celebrations on April 23 or playing the flute and with the keyboard in school parties. I think back to the countless Barbara Cartland romances I read, the knowledge contests I attended in middle and high school, all those opening speeches and presentations in school events, and the moment I made a whole stadium of students shout at the top of their lungs as I recited Ataturk's address to the Turkish Youth[1] on a May 19 celebration.[2] And of course, I will never forget my father's words: "You're going to be a very different girl; I will provide the best education that I can to you and make it possible for you to be sociable, outgoing, and different from others." This would become my earliest mind programming, and I still operate from that mind-set today; many thanks to my father, my glamorous galactic leader.

Ask anyone, and they will say that I was a happy child (and that I was definitely made of a different kind of stardust). When I think of myself, I am reminded of so many happy memories made by so many of my roles:

Sweet little Burcu, who took her baths in the lukewarm waters of the Mediterranean Sea; smart Burcu, who passed all her exams with straight As and who finished every year with letters of appreciation for her exceptional success records; ambitious Burcu, who was elected class president every year; creative Burcu, who won back-to-back poetry and essay-writing contests; involved Burcu, who made her family proud by being a part of the school band, the folk-dance club, the sports club, and the social club; accomplished Burcu, who was always among the best and the most promising students; dedicated Burcu, who liked to study; social Burcu, who was as smart as she was popular; beautiful, brunette Burcu, who was always skillful and resourceful.

Well, it sounds pretty awesome up until here, right? As if she's a shining stardust from her birth. Yes, my story

---

[1]   The legacy speech that Ataturk speaks to the Turkish youth about how they should live their life, protect their country and honor their republic.

[2]   National holiday for Turkey; May 19 The Commmemoration of Ataturk and Youth and Sports Day

begins and goes on beautifully like this. But actually, what can I tell you? These are just some of the experiences that filled the first 16 years of my life. With all these success stories as a teenager behind me, I was waiting for the rest of my life (especially the last three years of it).

The tiny living space of Anamur was very narrow for me; I had a much broader vision, and I knew I was supposed to live a bigger life. By 16, I had already done everything that I could in Anamur. Despite the many discoveries I made about myself, I was at the height of my youth. I knew I wanted to do the things I saw my peers doing on TV. I wanted to go to the movies and to the theater. I want to travel and have different experiences. After all, I had already counted all the stars in my sky; I wanted to look at other Shiny skies too. I wanted to have my freedom, fly with the strength of my own wings, and challenge the wind. I wanted to recreate myself. Instead of the life that had been given and offered to me, I wanted to experience a very different life, and by extension, a very different me—and on my own terms!

When I flew away from Anamur, there was no cinema, no theatre, not even a café. Even the youth magazines came very belatedly there. Of course, there was also no Internet back then. The only things that connected me to the world were television and radio. My favorite show on TV was (of course), the legendary *Beverly Hills 90210*. I got lost in the fantasy of those giant streets with tall palm trees as well as the colorful, vivacious, exciting, and glamorous lives they all lived, so full of options and freedom. I was definitely attracted to a life like that. I remember saying to myself, "One day, I am going to live in a place like that!" That magical sentence was a summary of my dream life. I spoke to the deepest levels of my heart, my stardust, and I knew that I would make the dream my reality—one day.

For that freedom, I worked very hard. I worked with all the university preparation books and magazines. I attended special courses and took pilot tests for the real university exam. I studied all the time—even at picnics or while I was watching soccer games on TV with my father. I was focused on the target: I had to be very successful in the university exam so I could get rid of this little life.

And I did it!

My first stop was Ankara. I wished to get rid of that little life and find myself a place in a big city. Since I didn't have many other alternatives to do in my limited life, I knew I needed to create the opportunities I needed to get ahead. When I was just 16, I was accepted to the international relations department of Middle East Technical University in Ankara. METU is known as the MIT of Turkey. I won a scholarship from the prime ministry. Think about it—how big my pain must have been to get away from it. I experienced that construction in my life at an international level. While wishing to study at the university, I was also unconsciously creating the option for living abroad. (Well, I do really rock!)

METU was a very good place for me to be. I engaged myself with the many activities that my heart desired, from *pas de deux* classes to the basketball team, from radio club to the step dance team! I danced, I jumped, I ran, I made my own radio show, and I got a championship medal on the basketball team. I lived freely as myself. I've created a new Burcu who was different and talented, just like my father had predicted when he put the code in me when I was very young.

To be honest, there was a slight difference. The Burcu I created wasn't exactly the Burcu my father wanted me to be. My version was a little too free-spirited and rebellious for his tastes.

Because of the differences between me at 16 versus me at 20, some serious problems emerged between my father and me. A few elements came together to create this perfect storm of conflict between father and daughter. When you combined the fierce blood of the fire of youth that burned in my veins—the endless enthusiasm I felt as a result of the freedom I now enjoyed—with the darkening of my father's inner world (together with the perception I had back then), my perception of who my father really was began to blur.

I was at a loss to understand how on Earth my dear daddy—the one who encouraged (and manipulated) me to be "different" when I was very little, who combed and braided my hair when I was going to school, who installed an audio system in the house and insisted that I play and sing songs, and who encouraged me to enjoy and make other people happy—could now possibly blame me with "not knowing any boundaries." How could he not speak with me for weeks, even months? How was it even possible that he reacted this way after teaching me to think freely and to be original? Was it because I had decided (with the free will he insisted I had) I didn't want to be a diplomat? Was it because I wanted to go live in Istanbul and work in the communications sector? I'm not sure, but my father reacted with a great opposition, even to the point of not even coming to my graduation ceremony.

He really wanted me to start working at the Ministry of Foreign Affairs, under the security and prestige of the government as a diplomat. I was then to become a consul, and in time, an ambassador who represented Turkey. He wanted me to have a red passport and to live that prestigious life (and make him live it too). I gave his dream a chance;

I did my internship at the ministry. But at the end of my internship period, I realized that the cost of being a part of the governmental structure involved the death of my big dreams. I wanted to live a free, international life and do what I want and what I have been waiting to do since my childhood. What I really wanted was to go live in a bigger city (Istanbul, to be more specific). I wanted to work with the talents and character traits I've discovered. Working in the communication sector was one way, I "Be-Lived" I could reflect my own light within.

And of course, my darling, as a rebellious spirit who has tasted the delicious chocolate cake of freedom, I did what I wanted to do!

This was one of the hardest periods of my life. I had stood against my father and thrown myself into the challenges of a big city, Istanbul, without any means and devoid of my father's financial and emotional support. I was focused on a new target: Doing anything and everything to get a job in the biggest international advertising agency in Istanbul. First, I prepared my résumé and sent it. After that, I called them and demanded a meeting. They said that they could not have a meeting with every single candidate that called them. And then I asked them, "But you wouldn't turn someone down if that person came to your door, would you?" And since I was satisfied with the answer I received, right after putting the phone down, I actually got up and rushed to see them. That's the persistent 🌟 side of me! After a difficult time getting in, I was nagging a man in the HR department, saying, "I'm newly graduated from METU. Give me a chance." A woman who must have heard my words while passing entered the room. After chatting for a short time with me, she said, "I'm seeing my youth in you. Come start your internship with me. You'll help me with the events I'm conducting and you'll

6

learn the job." With this sentence, my advertising career started, my dear sky princess... ⭐⭐⭐⭐

So I did what I came to do and found myself a job in a big advertising company, but the hardships coming my way continued without any interruption, too. It was as if life was testing my faith. For many long years, I couldn't find my identity—who I wanted to be. I had various problems with many different people. I got gastritis, a known side effect of advertising business, and that side effect proceeded to the beginning of ulcer. By working in three different advertising agencies in three years, I also broke a personal record of change, as well. ⭐ Thank God I had my mother. She always supported me. Because she was a financially independent woman who had seized one of the opportunities that life presented her and become a teacher, she was working and making her own money. And although she didn't approve of my decisions, she always supported her little girl. Those were the days that I first realized that for personal freedom in life, financial freedom was essential. No matter what, I had to take my mother as an example for myself to always make my own money, without depending on anyone else! With this decision in my mind, I focused on strengthening the order that I created, by doing my job well and enjoying it while I was doing it, and simply creating my own comfort zone.

Until one day I got a new intern that had just come from Los Angeles after two years and completed a certification program at UCLA Extension! This information immediately stuck in my mind like the stickiest note 3M ever produced. "Yes!" my neurons screamed inside of me. "Haven't you always wanted to live there? Look, LA is calling you, baby! Come on, go for it!" And an irresistible dazzling feeling of freedom captured my whole soul! In the midst of all these ebbs and flows and drifting I was experiencing, taking off to the city of my dreams and waking up every morning with the legendary golden sunshine of California was definitely looking like a GALACTIC idea!

And of course, the next stop was Los Angeles....

But how was I to cover all the expenses for my education, accommodations and life expenditures? I have many memories where I feel myself like a princess in little Anamur; where my family provided me with the best of everything. Starting from my childhood, we would specifically go to Mersin or Ankara, bigger cities where we can find the greatest brands, just to do our annual fashion shopping. I was 17 when I first went to England for a summer school, 18 when I went to Spain with Work and Travel and only 21 when I had a brand new car. But at this time, I was living a life that my father didn't approve of, and it was impossible to get his approval for such a budget. Therefore, creating a formula for my dream to experience life in United States took 1.5 years, my dear Stardust! One and a half years!!! That's 18 months!

And while I was planning how I could go to United States, NLP entered my life. I remember it very well. In 2003, my brother gave me a book and said to me, "This is just for you." I read it and I was impressed. I wanted to learn more about it, but at that point I wasn't able to foresee that NLP would change the whole meaning of my life. It seemed to be a fabulous resource for what my father always told us: "Don't let your head ONLY complete the picture of your body. Make it work!" ⭐ But because I couldn't get live answers for the questions I asked from the book, I didn't quite understand what NLP really was. NLP training was expensive and I Be-Live'd that I could never attend with the money I was earning, so I didn't even bother myself with setting a goal for it. Therefore, it took nearly six years for me to understand what NLP is and realize that understanding it—understanding myself—would have made things so much easier! ☆ So, my dear stardust friend, that's why you should hear my words and first understand yourself. Don't make the mistake I did. Do not wait another day to go discover the magical mechanics of your brain! Learn NLP and find the answers to questions like: How does the mind work? How do my behaviors take shape? What is the secret for a healthy communication? What is life? What does it mean to BE YOU?

I was still reading my NLP books, not neglecting my personal development in my own way, while still trying to find a way to go to LA. And since I wasn't able to get an approval from my father, I created my own solution that I could afford and applied as an au pair. And guess what? I got accepted by a family in Santa Monica. In January 2004, I made it to the United States to live my 90210 dreams! Yeah, baby. This is how you do it! ☆ First we went to New York in the really cold winter, which seemed like traveling to the Ice Age, and got babysitting education with the other au pair friends from all over the world. Then we were sent to the cities where the family we would with work lived. So, here I was in the City of Angels, where the broad Pacific shores reside.

Naturally, after seeing the charm of the tall palm trees, and the UCLA campus that was amazing, green and full with colorful flowers and hundreds of thousands of foreign students studying there, I couldn't stay there as a babysitter! After all, I was a METU (the MIT of Turkey) graduate and a person with four years of experience in the advertising business. What I actually wanted to do in the United States was to study! Especially at UCLA! Those who have been to Los Angeles would know that UCLA campus is very close to Santa Monica. Without traffic, you can be in the campus within seven minutes. But the American woman I was working for was telling me how far away their house was from the school, and that I should just not go. I perceived these ridiculous statements as an insult to my high IQ. And because of that I had serious problems with the family. I told them that my purpose was never to be a babysitter and left that place immediately! And with the thought that I might as well be studying at UC Berkley, I went to San Francisco to live with another family. Oh, my. I wish I never did that!

Now, Sky Power, I want you to imagine the house I went to live in—packed with cats, cold and dark and in a totally remote part of the city— in fact, remote to the life and to the world. And you had to see the room they gave me! Oh, my!!! A narrow, dark room with a squeaking bed and lots of cat stink in it, it was a terrible place! My God! When I saw that room that I don't even want to remember, I told myself in tears, "What the heck am I doing here?" and I went back first to Los Angeles and then impulsively back to Istanbul.

But I already had decided that this journey would have a fantastic comeback! This stop was only a break, because this traveler had to be on her way, baby!

As soon as I got back to Istanbul, I made a crisis evaluation and arranged a temporary job for myself in order to maintain myself during the period where I would get my TOEFL (Test Of English as a Foreign Language) score and wait for the approval from UCLA. This time, I had started my journey with a much bigger aim, and by explaining the big advantages it would create for me if I could study in United States day and night, I was even able to get the permission from my daddy! Yaay! After all, there was a half-told story, and my aim was to get an international education. Because one of my father's personal mottos was, "Whatever you do, do it fully," he Be-Live'd that I could complete this American adventure with a good education. But according to our agreement, my parents would only be covering my educational costs. My accommodation costs and all other life expenses would be my responsibility. They would pay the fee for the courses I took at UCLA and wouldn't pay for anything else. I had no idea know how I could take such a big risk, but even this agreement was the most exciting news on the world for me. I started the preparations for a new adventure with great enthusiasm. I started thinking about how I can create a financial resource for myself and managed to do it in a fantastic way by selling my Sports International membership that I had bought one year ago when I had a decent salary!!! And with that resource, I was rich, my dear! ☆ And the result: I was throwing myself to America one more time, with only $900 in my pocket! And my mood was like, "I'm not afraid of you my dear life. Bring it on. Show me your pearls!" ☆

In September 2004, I set foot to Los Angeles again as a UCLA Extension student, in order to finish my half-written story and if possible, to make it a "happy ending" this time. So I threw myself once again into a great unknown with $900 in my pocket and a great courage inside me. When I went through customs and entered the United States through Tom Bradley International, a brand new journey had already started! And Be-Live it or not, my Stardust, when I was out of the airport, I didn't have a place to stay, or a job to work at or solid money to ensure my path ahead. And even though I've studied at METU, which is an American-inspired public school with English education, the English I hear in United States was very different! And because I didn't know anybody except my other au pair friends in LA, that hotel where one of my Brazilian au-pair friends stayed and bartered her bill in exchange for working at their front desk was almost a miracle for me. I knew that the fact I had heard about that hotel and visited it before was not a coincidence at all. Again, I knew very well that this hotel would be only a beginning for me! And I would create my own cosmic life with my own determination and tenacity from there on!

And that's what happened, my dear cosmic princess. I went to that hotel directly from the airport, checked into a room, and said that I would work at the front desk in return for staying. When there was a place and my turn came, I would also start to work in the restaurant of the hotel and earn my money this way. But the hotel was a totally international one, so I had to speak to people from all over the world and understand all kinds of accents and dialogues—even the ones that sounded to me like chirping birds! Here I was, astonishing the clients with my own accent and the sentences I could build very slowly, and look what kind of a job I had found for myself! So I started to work at the front desk of that hotel, with a dictionary in my hand and a smile on my face that hid my hesitation.

I also learned which bus was going to my school and started to transform my room in the hotel into a library and—when my new friends from school started to visit me in my place—Into a very joyful and exotic living space. I was doing my homework with great joy. I was feeling that the more I used English, the better I could express myself. And then one day, something happened that changed my life in America entirely, as if it was a miracle!

One morning, I was drinking tea with my friends and I left the cafeteria to go get something in my room. A man around his mid-forties, with a luminous face and smiling eyes, who charmed me with the gleam of his bald head and darling belly, stopped me and asked me if I was Turkish.

"Yes," I said. "I'm Turkish." He was an Iranian. Later on, I was to discover that there were many Iranians in Los Angeles, who came before or after the Iranian Revolution and became very successful here. In fact, most of the Iranians lived in the most beautiful neighborhood of LA, Beverly Hills 90210, which was the name of my favorite TV show in high school—and the fuel for my desire to live there. Anyway, while I was running through all these in my mind, that cute Iranian guy asked me what I was doing in Los Angeles. "I live in this hotel, work at the front desk and study at UCLA," I answered. He bestowed on me a very sincere smile, "I was watching you at the cafeteria and I understand from the way you talk and your laughter that you love your life a lot and I liked it," he said. "Here. Take my card and call me. I'll change your life." I took the card with a great astonishment, much excitement and, of course, very well deserved doubt, and went on my way. My mind was speaking different languages inside and I said to myself, "Oh, my God! I just had a scene out of a real American movie!!! What is happening? Who is that guy? What does he want from me? Why did he tell me to call him? How will he change my life? Is he a pervert or what? Is he a porn movie producer?" I had thousands of thoughts in my head. He didn't seem like a troubled man, though. On the contrary, he seemed to be very sweet-natured and affectionate, and he created very "friendly" feelings in me. But I didn't have anybody to protect me if anything went wrong. No mom or dad, no big brother, no friends and relatives. I was all alone there. I was astonished by this event. Because I do Be-Live in miracles ever since my childhood! I always thought that one day something would happen and my whole life would change. And I also expected that to happen, too.⭐ So this could have been a miracle!!! But what kind of a miracle was it? Can you imagine how would you feel, if you were me, my dear stardust? It was something that would totally freeze the human brain and make you say, "What the f...?" What would you do if you were me? Would you say to yourself, "Is he a lunatic or pervert? What does he want from me?" Or would you say that you Be-Live in miracles like me and call that guy that very evening? ⭐

Yes, I trusted my feelings and immediately called him, cosmic beauty.⭐ I chose to Be-Live that he was a gift from God to me and with the warm feelings I saw in his eyes, and I met with him. You must be wondering what happened, right? Well, yes, he really changed my life! It was incredible. It was a real miracle that a person like him was alive on this planet! His name was Anoosh and it is in hundreds of hearts. First he found me a second job where I could work and earn more money, a Persian restaurant as a waitress where I made good money with the tips.⭐After that he bought me a car so I could easily go to my school, and later a laptop so I could do my homework nicely. And he was incredible enough to schedule my debt to him on a monthly basis, according to my earnings. Can you Be-Live it, my cosmic darling? And then, he turned to me and said, "Welcome to America, Burcu! There's nothing for free here, my dear! I'm doing this to give you the notion of responsibility, and in return I want only one thing: Do the same thing to other people." ⭐ This was totally a sentence that my dad could have said, as if a little different version of my father has found me here in America and he was taking care of me. It was unbelievable! But it was happening, my lovely. ⭐ I was utterly amazed and feeling grateful that there are still these kinds of people in the world and one had found me!! How blessed I was to be able to attract such an angel into my life? I was realizing that

I was experiencing an incredible miracle and I was feeling almost "chosen" because I met a person like him.

By the way, as you know, my darling stardust, if you don't have a Social Security number in the United States, or if your credit score is below 600, American banks would not give you a credit card or credit. At that point, I had a Social Security number because in my first visit to America I was here with J1 visa at the request of the family I was working for, and I got myself a Social Security number right away. But I didn't have a credit history under this number. I wasn't reliable financially and I didn't have any financial assurance that I could submit. So I didn't have a credit score at that time. That meant that being able to pay for my car and laptop in monthly installments was an easy payment for me. And I was ready to take this responsibility and do anything and everything on the way to my purpose, working day and night!

So a real miracle had happened and an angel with all the love in his heart had entered my life. His name was Anoosh but he wanted me to call him Anooshjoon (a diminutive suffix in Persian language), and he was a true friend, a mentor, a light and a guardian angel. In Anooshjoon's life, the good deeds he performed didn't start or end with me. When I was added to his circle of love, he had already picked hundreds of people according to their energy levels, just like he picked me. For some he found jobs, to others he taught how to drive a car and with some, he worked on as a mentor—just like he did for me—and taught them the ways to succeed in America. I had the honor of enhancing the ethnic repertoire of that Godly man who undertakes it as a duty to guide and be the light in the lives of people from many different countries, from Russia to Ethiopia, from France to Iran, from Mexico to Venezuela and especially to young women like me, who came here from the other end of the world, all alone pursuing a dream. ⭐I was only to discover that a Russian girl named Marina, *with whom I worked at the same hotel and appreciated her determination,* was also under the wings of Anooshjoon. ⭐Life is very weird, isn't it, my cosmic princess? For those of you who are searching and also Be-Live'ing, it is full of miracles. Trust me, my darling.⭐

And with the new page I opened with Anooshjoon, my America adventure had reached a very different level. At least twice a week I was going to his house, having conversations with other girls he invited, discovering different aspects of life and also laughing and having a lot of fun too. With the help of the fabulous banquet of home-cooked, special Persian dishes, different music and songs we sang together and games we played with each other, I was feeling as if I'd found a real American family for myself each time I went there. But I also have to share with you my working tempo, especially after the start of the school, when my expenses went higher and higher, my dear cosmic beauty:

The first waitress shift in the hotel was in 5 – 7 a.m., and I jumped on that opportunity right away. I was waking up before dawn to prepare breakfast for the guests of the hotel. After finishing my shift, I would go to my other job to the other restaurant. After finishing there, I would take a shower and going to school. No, this tempo wasn't tiring me. But as a person who was in the first 100 in the university exam, won METU and worked the following four years in the biggest international advertising agencies in the world and managed communication campaigns for very big brands, placing the breakfast plates to the dishwasher seemed insulting. It was crashing my ego down, as if the problems I had encountered in order to belong to the "communication" world in Istanbul wasn't enough. I was feeling like my beautiful God has sent me to America on purpose, so that I would pay a bigger price for it. And when I think pf the things I had to do, I was making myself feel alone and desperate. Yes, I had encountered an angel like Anooshjoon, but still I was the one who had to do all these things to survive. I was the one who had to wake up in the wee hours, work together with those uneducated Mexicans and put aside my pride. When my 10-year-old car broke down in the middle of the night, I put aside my fears. I was the one who had to call a tow truck and pay for it. While I was focused on creating my comfort zone in Istanbul, it was also me who came here and had thrown herself to these hardships. Me and myself. Therefore, it was also me again who should confront these difficulties. For that reason I had to condone that my ego would hurt for a while as I focused on my target and worked in these kind of jobs until I finished my study and my work permit came. **"Come on, Burcu, stop whining. You chose this way. Focus on the target. Imagine the success and keep on going on your way!"**

And I did continue!

Also with the presence of Anooshjoon, my approach to life and people had begun to change and develop. His place and importance in my life as a psychology graduate mentor and a friend that I endlessly trusted had also begun to increase every day. He was explaining that I had to trust myself more, care about my talents more, specify a target, focus on it and increase my self-worth. He gave me advice on every subject to become successful in America, and he was investing a great amount of his time in me for my development. Anooshjoon belived in me since he first saw me in the hotel, and he wanted me to shine like a star and illuminate my own world. ☆

When I finally could check out of the hotel, I rented a room for myself in the house of an old lady. The first thing I did was to show it to him and share my happiness with him. Though I was so happy that I could take that step and create a more "normal" living space for myself, my expenses were doubled with the addition of the rent, so I had to raise the number of jobs I was working to three. And, of course, because the jobs I could work were limited with a student visa, I reevaluated my resources and chose again the babysitting option. This time I was lucky to work in a gorgeous house in Beverly Hills with the postal code of 90210—my dream city—for an American family that had two beautiful children.

When I look back now, I see what a great steadiness I've had and I want to applaud myself. Those were interesting days. I remember how embarrassed I felt when I shared the jobs I was was doing with a Turkish friend that I had met in an event organized by Los Angeles Turkish American Association. Yes it was very offensive for me and I couldn't handle it well, but I was Be-Live'ing that all of that would end, that I would graduate and find a job in an advertising agency. Customers who came to the restaurant wanted to chat with me because I always had a smiling face, but of course, they didn't know how hard I was working to show them that smiling face. The truth is always different than what you see from outside, my cosmic beauty. You know....

At the end, all of these difficulties really ended. I was graduated with the highest grades and took my diploma from the school I came here dreaming about. YAY! But the real exam was just yet to begin at that point. When my work permit came, I had already decided where I wanted to work and what I wanted to do. I had taken steps in that direction and with the mentality "I would do whatever it takes," I had managed to get what I wanted even on the other side of the world! Great job, Burcu! ⭐ You did it! ⭐ And listen to the story how I made it. It is really an extraordinary one.

In my last semester at UCLA, we had an IMC (Integrated Marketing Communication) course and we all loved the teacher of the course! His name was Robert Liljenwall and he was the cutest professor I saw in my life, the sweetest teacher and the loveliest personality in the world. In our text book, an advertising agency in Santa Monica was shown as a living example of IMC. And one day Robert said, "I know the founder of this agency. Would you like me to take you there for an evening?" Two weeks later, we were at the agency that then was the Phelps Group and now renamed Phelps Agency. I was excitedly listening to the story of Joe Phelps from the front row. As he explained the system he had built and the agency culture he had created, my jaw dropped more and more! As soon as Joe Phelps' presentation was over, I ran and caught him. "I'm graduating at the end of this semester and I have four years of work experience in advertising agencies in Turkey," I said. "I would love to work in this magnificent agency that you created and be a part of it." Joe looked at me and said, "Who are you?" I introduced myself. Joe was very surprised. He liked my self-confidence and loved that I was pursuing my desire, taking initiative on the subject and approaching him like that. "But," he said, "I'm not the one who makes recruitment decisions; you have to have three or four interviews and pass the presentation test." To that I answered, "I would do anything you want, I would even start as an intern. I just want to have an opportunity to have an experience here." After Joe, I had four more interviews and when I delivered the presentation they were expecting from me in such a short time and with such high quality that exceeded even their expectations, I got the job, baby! Yaay! ⭐ That was my incredible story.⭐

Ah, my dear Stardust, this is how life works. It's a game of specifying your target, focusing on it with all your cells and when you accomplish it, to specify a new target and go toward it! And while going toward a new target, experience new things about yourself. Yes or yes? ⭐

My next target was to get a work permit through the company and stay in America. For that, I was taking on all the work that I could do in the agency myself, working extra hours, creating exceptional results and going to Joe with those results. The reaction I got for the presentation I made to the Agency President Joe and Vice President Glenn made me feel so successful and happy that I had never experienced before! I got both a salary raise and also an approval of my working visa so that I could stay in America!!! Yaay! Birds! Butterflies! Yaay! Many times yaay! I did it again! I'm fantastic! I'm amazing!

In the meantime, I experienced the most miraculous encounter in my life when I was in Anamur on my vacation and met a very handsome guy. I saw him in the wedding pictures of a friend of a very close friend of mine in Los Angeles, and I was attracted immediately. My mom wished that I would meet someone like him, hold his hand and go back to Turkey with him! Yes, he came just like that, out of blue sky! Well, actually, not really. It was me again—my incredible law of attraction in action, which focused on the target and took action for him to come into my life. That was the reason I met him, but that's another story, my lovely. At the end of the story, there is a big love and a story of going back to Turkey after such a hard pursuit, effort and success in the American Dream. You see, my Stardust, after working that hard, shutting down the voice of my ego, reaching to my target, I left LA and followed the idea, *"Let's go back to Turkey, get married and start a family."* That's exactly what a Pisces would do.

And so the next stop was Istanbul again.

This stop was the period of my life where I truly hit the rock bottom and Be-Live'd that God was punishing me. I questioned the concept of "life" thoroughly with the most unbelievable tragedy I've ever gone through. The tragedy where I lost my joy of life, where I lost all the meanings that I had created and where I was devastated.

I had miraculously met with the guy I saw in a picture a year ago, fallen in love with him, gotten engaged to him and, just like my mother's wish, I flew back to Turkey in the same plane with him, hand in hand. Our plan was first to find jobs for both of us in Istanbul, then buy ourselves a nice house and then get married at the end of the summer. He had finished his master's degree and completed his internship, and I had received my diploma and gained work experience in America. With our new complements, we were very excited to start a brand new life! And we were looking forward to sharing this exciting news with our families! And since my family lived in Anamur, we made a plan to meet them in Ankara, in my brother's place. But my fiancé wanted me to stay in Istanbul for the first two nights, spending those days with his family, and then for me to go to Ankara. I wanted to go to Ankara right away, because I have missed my family so much and also I couldn't wait to share these beautiful emotions with them. *"Just stay for two nights," he said. "What will change in two nights?"* So we had a conflict there. I said to him that I wanted to consult my father. So I called my dad and explained the situation. I would never forget what my father told me: *"My dear daughter, he will be your husband. We can wait for two more days. You should please him.*" And I decided to do so. So we changed the plan. I was to stay in Istanbul for the first two days and my parents were to go to the Black Sea Region tour that my brother bought them as a gift. We were to meet with them at the end of the second day in Ankara. How could I know that it was the last conversation that I had with my daddy?☹

My mom called me the day after that magical night where we came back from America, and she said: "*Your father is not well. Don't go to Ankara, come here, to Trabzon immediately.*" We ran out of the house immediately and they delivered me to the airport. When I was about to buy my ticket to Trabzon, my mom called again: "*No, don't buy a ticket for Trabzon. I didn't know how to say it to you, but we lost your father because of a heart attack, yesterday evening.*" I remember screaming "NOOOOO!" in the middle of the airport and falling down to the ground and remaining there for an infinite number of moments.

I remember the moment I saw him lying down with his lifeless, cold body, with his closed eyes. Again I screamed at the top of my lungs, "WHY?" I screamed, "WAKE UP, DADDY!" And my dad did not wake up and did not embrace me. I remember truly understanding what it meant to DISSAPEAR from the earth. And while we were holding my daddy's funeral, I remember hundreds of cars on that interprovincial highway lined up back to back, in order to tell him his final goodbye. How the heck in the world, I was thinking, could so many people from that kind of a little town show up for my daddy? Who were they? How did my father get to know so many people and manage to have a place in their hearts? It was unbelievable. And unforgettable at the same time.

That image that I can never forget is still very vivid in my mind's eye. When we were very young, he always said, *"Before being anything else, be a decent human being. Respect others. Just respect."* And on that day, the whole population of his community approved all the values that made my father, my respected father, the one and only ESAT UNSAL! My dear daddy had accomplished much to have those values that he had and Be-Live'd after his departure! That was the legacy my father left me! To be a decent human being before everything and to make respect alive.

And thus became July 22, 2006, the date I started to question life deeply. My whole being was wrapped up with the pain of knowing that I wasn't able to create a healthy communication or deep connection with my father since my university years. That was the period of my life that I drained myself by asking, *"Why? Why? Why?"* and Be-Live'd that life was punishing me. A period where I felt all the mistakes I made, all the people I hurt knowingly or unknowingly inside myself and apologized. A period where I started a journey to celebrate life and a fresh new beginning but found only grief, where I hit the bottom of pain from the high peaks of happiness, that I didn't understand, that I didn't want to understand, that I didn't accept and revolted against. A period that was terrible, very tasteless and filled with nothingness. For months, I continuously read books, cried and slept. For months, I mourned for myself with my mother and at the same time tried to support her in those painful times as much as I could. The tragedy she was going through was deeper than any of our. They were so happy in that Black Sea trip; they traveled, they ate and drank with the group they went with, and even on the last night, my father took a microphone in his hand and explained to everybody how joyful he was. The next morning they were to come and meet us but my father never saw that morning. And my mom was with him, even when he couldn't open his eyes that night ...

Oh, my. All the great thinkers have said that someone who hasn't tasted death cannot live life fully, and in that tragic period of my life, I understood what they meant, my dear Stardust. One can only understand life and start to live it fully, after understanding that death is something very real and there is no turning back from it. And with the serious strike that this pain had hit me with, I understood I had to continue my life in order to fill the emptiness inside of me. I started to work in another big agency, Ogilvy, toward the end of that year.

Everything seemed so plain to me, yet I still had to play that "work hard and win in life" game. We had also started our marriage plans, and since my father was no longer with us, getting me married had become the most important duty of my mother. And on that too, I've encountered big and serious problems. I've experienced problems, fights and disagreements that I've never lived in my life before. I was already feeling hollow inside of me and with the addition of these problems; I took for the first time—and, thank god also for the last time—an anti-depression pill for a week in my life, my dear cosmic friend. We had planned to buy a house but we couldn't; we planned to be happier together and we couldn't. And the night before my wedding, I was in tears but I still got married. You may call it responsibility, you may call it being desperate, or an emotional need to hold on to something or maybe simply just hope. But I did get married. Then we started to "play" the marriage game: our friends were visiting us, we were visiting them back, we were taking nice vacations and traveling to Europe with friends. Yet there was always something artificial there.

Right around that time, the book The Secret became a hit and I became its number one fan, my cosmic dear. I was still questioning life, wanting to understand why all these things had happened to me, wishing to create a meaning and getting rid of this heavy burden I had been carrying on my shoulders. I was reading—reading a lot of books and asking myself what my father would do if he were in that kind of a situation. I started to have problems in the agency where I was working. The more I tried to become a better human being, the more I started to question the humanity of others. And then came the crises. I worked very hard and got many responsibilities, and yet I was not receiving enough or simply "fair" financial reward for my efforts! I wanted to quit my job. I didn't accept the injustice performed upon me and I was wondering why I couldn't hold onto jobs that I started, and wondering if I had a problem. In the pursuit of the problem in me, I started to look for NLP training for myself. I had a very intense business life, so I couldn't go to the training for years. I wanted to break the chains in me, to scream, but I couldn't do it. All those books I read had no answers to my questions! I tried again. I said to myself, "*OK, this time I'll definitely go to the training,*" and then I couldn't manage to go there again. I wasn't able to take time off from my job and I didn't want to use my annual leave for the training. So at the end, I didn't go.

Then I read a sentence by Einstein in a book: "*Insanity is doing the same thing over and over again and expecting different results.*" And I asked myself, "Am I insane?" I was experiencing all these problems in the advertising world, so I decided to go to the client side, to experience something new, and create and manage my own brand. And with that new decision to do something different, I gave my resignation. That's how the chain of CHANGE started for me, my stardust friend! First I finally went to the NLP training that I have been waiting for years to do and then I found a very high-quality C-level executive job on the client side with amazing benefits. And you know what? I felt so much creative expression, so much love and connection and so much ownership to that job that I was finally experiencing how my skills and my potential could make a huge difference for a big international organization like this one! I was the right hand for the CEO, I was managing a $70 million marketing budget with over 150 employees, I was traveling to Europe, and I was creating a real, measurable and drastic change for the company! It was an incredible feeling to experience my true potential, which I knew inside was even bigger than this!

I was aware that the first NLP training I went was a total baloney, far from the books and concepts of NLP that I learned. It was a total manipulation based on the SHALLOW worldview of the person who gave it. I was puzzled. So I started to search for REAL NLP TRAINING. I learned through the Internet that the founder of NLP was Richard Bandler and I wanted to learn NLP from his licensed NLP Trainers. Obviously, other unqualified wannabe NLP Trainers were everywhere. So I found the original source of Richard Bandler's licensed NLP trainers database (*where my name is now also listed as one of his legitimate, world-class NLP trainers in California, by the way*). The link is: <u>http://nlptrainers.com</u>, and I encourage anyone to visit it who is considering learning the world's number one technology of the mind from its real, original source! And at that time, in 2009, there was only one institution that was bringing licensed trainers from the Society of NLP, and they were opening courses only on demand, so they gave me a date for a year later. "OK," I said. "I will wait. Count me in." I gave the money in advance and I enrolled, just like that. I was that determined to learn NLP from the original source, ask my questions to the trainer, and program my mind to reach my full potential!

Meanwhile at my new job, serious problems were occuring between me and one of the company advisors. I was struck by his dark thoughts and unethical quick wit. But we were taking super new steps for the company together and we were great at the new vision and planning areas. I explained to him the brilliant work culture of the agency at which I worked in America and that its founder was getting continuous executive trainings at Harvard. For such a global vision we were trying to create, this kind of a global education was absolutely mandatory, I said. The advisor's eyes were shining so bright when he heard that idea and he immediately said, "Then we should include an extensive higher education at Harvard Business School for all the executives in our annual plan!" Just like that, I was off to experience another dream in my life, all sponsored by the company that I worked for my intergalactic nebula dust! And six months later, we were in Boston, as an executive group of nine people, learning the state-of-the-art strategies to become better leaders for our organization and to learn the best practices to lead our industry, my Stardust. It was just like I dreamed and also felt in my heart that I was also going to get my executive education from Harvard, when I first heard that our CEO was attending Harvard Business School to take his company to the next level, in 2005. It was only four years later that I was living my dream, my Shiny one! ☆ So Be-Live in your dreams!

Harvard Business School's Executive Education was the hardest education process of my life. Between all the homework, working groups, researches, essay readings and presentations, I remember losing 10 pounds in one week! You see, my sparkly, everything has a price to pay. On top of all that, the problem between the advisor and me got a lot worse during the Harvard education period. While we were discussing about an assignment, he threatened me in the broad daylight, in front of all those people, because I expressed my different opinion that didn't quite support his opinion and, most importantly, because all of our executive team adopted the idea I suggested! It was unbelievable! There I was, getting an education in the best school in the world, living my dream and enjoying a very big opportunity in my hands, and all I was thinking was to complete my assignments properly and get my diploma, but I was also dealing with the big fluffy ego and irrational, unbelievable threats of that guy! Oh, my! Oh, my! This is how the human nature shows up, my darling. You gotta watch out for jealous attacks and be smart all the time!

Of course, when we were back, I made sure that justice was served and the advisor was fired, my galactic fireball. And I started to work even closer with our CEO. And guess what, my dear. This time, the inflated egos of the managers of other countries started a war against me and my position! Those were the days that I wasn't able to work just because I had to deal with a different ego problem every single day, and inside myself, I had started to ask questions again. I really loved my job and how I made a huge difference for the company, and I was feeling that by concentrating on solving our internal communication problems before the mass communication of my brand, I was creating the fundamentals for a more flexible and a more interactive company culture. And I was totally aware that I was a pioneer leader of change, both as the head of marketing and also as the leader for the organizational development. I had even created the concept of "Heartbeats" for a New Year's party that I organized, giving little, sparkling hearts to all of the employees from five different countries, including our CEO, and even writing a poem that both celebrated and motivated our people. The poem was full of emotions, and we used it on the invitation cards that we designed for the party. It was a fabulous organization that increased both the motivation and the sales figures due to its intense emotionally bonding nature. And in the preparations of this organization, I worked one more time with all my power, had sleepless nights and again lost about 5 pounds because I couldn't eat anything. But I can't even start to describe the joy I felt when I reached my goal and saw those Shiny happy people who were both having fun and working with great motivation! That was true fulfillment and self-actualization my cosmic friend! That was an incredible feeling of accomplishment!

What I was starting to understand was the source of this joy. This joy was far beyond doing my job good. It was a more satisfactory, more meaningful and bigger joy. It was a wonderful thing that made me feel really special and important and made me experience the taste of being me. Something that made me Be-Live in myself more. When I think about it now, it is fascinating to realize how I came up with my brand and my message Be-Live in U in 2010! My favorite office accessory was my business cardholder that said "Believe" on it. ☆And I didn't know back then that I was actually programming my subconscious mind about my own brand and my message to the world today. It was happening because I was looking at it every day. Isn't that crazy?

At this time of my life when I was climbing the ladder of my career with huge steps, a natural financial and emotional distance started to build up at home between my husband and me. Because I was a smart, go-getter and attractive Turkish woman who was coded by her father to be "different" in her early childhood, with a great educational background and proven professional success records, I was "too much" for my husband's family. I chose not to be in touch with them, so he saw his family on the weekends when I was abroad for my business trips. It was not an ideal marriage structure, as you can imagine, my lovely. Plus, since I had left all my American dreams in order to get married and start a family with him, and I had stayed my first night with his parents on my return to Turkey and I was not able to see my father one last time, it affected my feelings about them. Of course, there's a reason for everything in life. It had to happen that way. Who could have known it? This was nobody's fault but a decision that life made. But back then this was how I was thinking, secretly blaming him inside. Also, I still had a deep longing for America inside of me and I was still debating if I should go back to Los Angeles. So I sat down and talked to my husband, but he didn't want to come with me. I decided to take a vacation to Los Angeles for three weeks with two of my girlfriends I had met there and become closer to in Istanbul to observe myself. Being in the City of Angels and living among the wide, well-kept, gorgeous natural beauties and sparkling life was like living in another dimension. There was still something that was attracting me to LA, something that I couldn't understand. I came back, heaving a lot of sighs after that vacation.

Right around that time, I heard from my beloved Anil Alpay, whom met in my life's Harvard period and for who I still have a deep gratitude for, that an Italian past-life regression therapist was coming to Istanbul. Anil told me much about dear Prem Shola, so I made my appointment with her months in advance! Sunday, May 16, 2010. I will never forget that date. It is the date of the beginning of my cosmic life. Because I have read so many books and attended countless seminars on spirituality, ancient wisdom and cosmic life, I knew exactly what to expect from that session! I knew my questions to be answered in my session with Shola: Why my father just went and left me like that, and why I didn't have closure four years after his passing. Why I was feeling such a big emotional connection and magnetic pull toward Los Angeles. And, most importantly, what my real mission in this life was.

OH, MY GOSH! I've never felt myself this close to you before, my Shiny god! What an experience it was! My consciousness was open and recording all the noises of the cars and the birds but I had lost the control of my body. I imagined my father as a green avatar and made the last conversation with him that I had to do. I got the last message that I needed to take from him. Moreover, I've learned that in my old life, which was steering my current life, I was an awesome Hindu goddess. At the end of the session, I was totally blown away! The goddess of knowledge, music and art. Let me introduce myself to you, my cosmic stardust. I am Saraswati. My mission as Saraswati was to share this fabulous light that I had with the whole world and illuminate humanity with my being! And I was to do this by telling stories. My first thought was, "But I already do this every day by telling stories to people I work with and share things in my presentations. So what is the meaning of this 'share your light' thing? How was I to do this?" I got some tarot readings and the session was repeated one week later. I left Shola with the most life-changing and valuable information I have ever heard in my entire life that still guides me in my journey today. This awakening on who I really was inside my core was such a true treasure for me that I knew my life would never be the same again! Literally, something had gone inside of me to awaken the goddess within me and after that, I was UNSTOPPABLE, baby!

Right after that spiritual awakening, I also had an intellectual awakening. Because the time for that NLP training that I wanted to take for a long time had also come! So I took my second NLP training in Istanbul from an English NLP trainer who had a Bandler license. Oh, my. The exercises we did have affected me deeply and in that very short period of time I've discovered many things that I didn't know about myself! For example, I discovered what I don't know about "human nature"! Very critical things indeed! I discovered that I didn't know so many things about myself and my communication style, even as a professional in the world of communication for 10 years with proven success records. And I discovered that those things that we don't know and are not aware are the things that affect our relationships, our thoughts, our feelings and the results we get in life the most! Immensely! And that I could actually reach my targets I've specified, if I really wanted. I remember screaming out loud when I thought one by one about the targets I've set for myself and reached just because I wanted them so much! Actually I have realized a very simple truth but it was like discovering a new planet for me. I had a big excitement in me and all the pieces of the puzzle were falling into their places. I still had many, many questions though. This awakening that started with Shola started a desire in me to read more about and understand NLP even more deeply. And of course, this time I was going to go study NLP with the mind who created it! With Dr. Richard Bandler! Furthermore, another friend of mine that I liked very much was attending the NLP training with me, and she had also become a very different source of inspiration for me by telling me about the Tony Robbins seminar she went in the United States in such an appealing way! I was sold to the idea right away! I wanted to go to United States immediately and have this education in its original place, join to the seminar of Tony Robbins and lose myself in it. And when I Googled, it I discovered fantastic things about it! Hey, Los Angeles, wait for me! I'm coming! ⭐

On June 21, I sat down and talked about all these things with my husband and tried to explain him this irresistible "calling" I was feeling in me once again. I told him, "Let's go back to Los Angeles. There's something calling me there. I can't stay with this feeling here anymore, I want to go!" He reacted in a very big way. Because he struggled a lot in the United States before, he didn't have the courage to deal with the same hardships again. His fears were stopping him. I told him, "Then let me go and stay there for six months. I'll try to understand what it is that is calling me there. Maybe you'll come later. Let's see." But sadly his focus was not trying to understand what I was going through and create a solution. Instead, his only focus was what he would say to everybody if I leave him and go to United States all by myself! Can you see the learned helplessness here, my Stardust? And do you wonder what did? Well, on September 16, 2010, I left my husband, my job where I was at my shining peak with many international travels and earning a great deal of money, my house, my belongings, my family, my friends— in short, my COMFORTABLE LIFE that I had carefully created after all these efforts. And yes, I opened my eyes in Los Angeles as a divorcée in pursuit of my COSMIC LIFE! ⭐

This time, I had more money in my pocket⭐, benefits of the corporate life and having a good job so I could save some money. Yes, it was more but it would only allow me to live there only for seven or eight months. Now, being me has become an expensive thing darling, you know? ⭐ And this time I wasn't alone either, because my friend whom I had met in LA and gotten close to to and later visited LA with came, too. Our plan was to stay with our beloved American family, with Anooshjoon until we found ourselves a home and new jobs and start a brand new life! It was as if God whispered to us, "Go on. It's your time to shine!" At least this was how I was feeling in the first months! You know why? Listen how the universe supported me in this spiritual journey: In our second week I found myself a super job as a marketing and branding consultant that I could work from home. In our third week, we had found a cute little apartment that satisfied us both and moved in. And within a month, I was already attending to my NLP training that I signed up for way before when I was in Istanbul!

At the NLP training, through the people I met, I was introduced to Kabbalah, the notion of metaphysics, Toastmasters and, most importantly, my own highest values! After the training, I had already convinced a friend that I met there to buy tickets together for Tony Robbins' seminar the following year, enrolled to study Kabbalah's spiritual teachings, became a member of Toastmasters in order to learn the secrets of becoming a good speaker and had already started my second bachelor degree, my masters and my PhD plans in metaphysic psychology! I was soul searching and hungry for all the information and teachings about life and myself! I was going to every seminar and investing in any kind of training that was teaching me something new about myself. I was determined to work on my mission to enlighten people, as a soul who lived her previous life as a goddess in this planet!

March 2011 became a turning point for my search of my new identity and the changes I've created in my life. I went to Miami to attend Tony Robbins' UPW (Unleash the Power Within) Seminar, and I came back as a totally different person. I quit smoking and quit drinking all fizzy, acidic drinks, especially Diet Coke. I understood what I wanted to do for the rest of my life. And I have proved to myself that the power within me was sharp enough to prevent me from feeling the hot burning coal under my feet! Yes, I had walked on the fire with Anthony Robbins and I had become a proud firewalker! And within the same month I went to Florida again, but this time to Orlando, to study Charisma Development and Trainer Training Program and became Richard Bandler's licensed NLP trainer. When I was back in Los Angeles, I realized that I was the first Turkish NLP trainer in the whole United States who got her license personally from Dr. Richard Bandler! It was so amazing! And I started to feel an incredible excitement to share this life-changing mind programming technology first with my own country and then with the whole world!

But of course, since I didn't know how to do it and where to start, the first thing I did was to knock on the doors of other institutions that were already giving NLP training. All the institutions wanted to train their own trainers and of course they weren't doing it for free, my dear. They wanted me to go through their NLP education, too, and pay twice the money a regular participant would pay! Ah, America, you're something! This is how you make someone to pursue her dreams. Because my dream was already to create my own business and to be independent, and because I knew that I had a lot of strengths, skills and talents, I had to say, "Well, then, I'll create everything myself and organize my own trainings!" I had to get ready for this! I was already studying at the University of Metaphysics, and I already got my license and was working towards my master's degree. I had gone to Tony Robbins' seminar and bought all of the programs he had ever created and started to work on them like crazy. Every day, every single day, I was working on a different CD or DVD of Tony Robbins. While I was illuminating my inner world with them, I was also analyzing how he used NLP in his own programs. It was a terrific internal journey! Every new day came with new awakenings, and in the evenings Kabbalah was explaining it spiritually. My whole psychology was being explained in the metaphysical world. It was a truly magical period of my life!!! 2011 in my personal history was the year of my TRANSFORMATION. ⭐ I was programming myself to be a better version of myself in every seminar, training, book, CD and DVD I could find. I don't remember any other time in my life that I studied with such a delight, such an "openness" and looked forward to understand everything, including my time at Harvard Business School!!

And, of course, because I was in the United States for a short time, I couldn't trust my English would be enough to give NLP trainings to Americans. I had my fears that stopped me: How the in the world I could find people and who could I find? If you think that these questions, insecurities and second-guessings would disappear after a while, you're wrong, my darling. We were living together in the same brain with these little voices, and we always carry them in our heads, wherever we go. ⭐ So only when we get enough knowledge, consciousness, competence and confidence we can come to a point where we can manage those voices the way we want to. ⭐ Then I raised the volume of another sound in my head and said, "I'm an NLP teacher! I can reach my goals by using NLP techniques and, of course, I can create a solution for me!" And that was what I did, my dear cosmic beauty. I used the very NLP techniques that I teach today in my trainings, organized my thoughts and fears, managed their sounds in my head and gave my first training in November 2011, in Istanbul Bilgi Paylasim Derneği[3]! ⭐ Four very sweet ladies came to my training. ⭐ I will be grateful for those four magical people who made me officially an NLP trainer until the end of my life! As I taught, my confidence became stronger and I had proved to myself that I could do this knowledge sharing work. ⭐ Oh la la la! ⭐

I started to take steps as soon as I went back to Los Angeles. First, I knocked on the door of UCLA. But if you remember how I started my advertising career, you might also guess how I knocked that door, too.⭐ UCLA Extension, where I was a student, was and is the number one in the world with the certificate programs about professional development, and it was only a few minutes away from me. When I thought about the idea to give NLP trainings at UCLA, all the stars in the sky came down into my eyes and started to shine from within with all the electrical charge they had! And, of course, I used my own method again; first send an e-mail, then call them, then call them again, and again, until I get what I want. And here I was again, at the door of UCLA! This time, I was chasing the director of the management department. ⭐Well, this story is really fun to share, because I was in his Inbox every single day with dissertation-long emails. ⭐ And he knew he had to see me or I was not going to stop. ⭐ And when I went to see him, he didn't even

---

[3] Istanbul Knowledge Sharing Association.

know that we were going to have a meeting.⭐ I kinda requested him, very persistently, by waiting at his door all day. ⭐ So just like that, my lovely, he gave me only five minutes to explain myself and my dream to him. And at the end of four minutes, I was already done explaining why I was an incredible instructor for UCLA and offering him an idea to organize an NLP certificate program at UCLA Extension. And he very kindly told me that they would call me back should there be any fit to my skills. You know how it works.⭐ And, yes, they did call me a few months later and asked me if I wanted to teach Leadership Communication Strategies course for UCLA Extension! ⭐ OH, MY GOSH!!! I was like, YES YES YES! Why do you even ask, right? ⭐ I was jumping in the air with joy and, boy, I had made it again!

So that's how I started to teach Leadership Communication Strategies course in the summer of 2012. My strategy of being laser focused and waiting at the door—if that was what it took—had worked once again! YES! I remember it so well. They called me to break this ultimate news on February 22, 2012, right after my birthday, my cosmic star. ⭐ And I remember how my mom couldn't believe that I was teaching at UCLA, until I gave my first class and sent her a picture of it. ⭐

After this news, I immediately organized a weekend seminar and made preparations for myself. My goal was to start teaching NLP to little groups to gain confidence for my new profession at UCLA and to became more comfortable with my English. At the same time, I also started to make contacts with educational institutions in Turkey and sold my training solutions for them, too. And I was still a student. UCLA was educating us trainers with great care and giving us mandatory trainings, as well as allowing us to participate in any course we wanted in order to support our professional development. Therefore, I participated every single psychology and communication course I possibly could. At the conferences I attended, I learned the most recent research studies about positive psychology, neuroscience and best practices as a change agent. I know very well that this adventure of being a student would continue for the rest of my life, dear. As you learn more, you realize how little you actually know. Filling the 100 billion cells in my brain with the knowledge that I wanted to learn wasn't actually only development or joy of "being"; but also was an irreplaceable freedom, my dear Northern Star! ☆Because with the knowledge—aka the programming—that I carefully chose, I was able to design the new ME! With all this illuminated knowledge and the choices I made with awareness, I was able to create a lot more COSMIC version of myself. A shinier one!

Do you know what happens when you are able to be yourself freely, my galactic superstar? Well, you live your dreams. ☆Becoming a motivational speaker was my next dream. And boom! There I was the very next year in 2013, rocking the stage with my speech on Be-ing yourself! And on April 10, 2014, as my cosmic version of myself, as a speaker at a huge conference in Istanbul! I was also experiencing the joy of returning the favor of my director Van Anderson, who couldn't resist my incredible teaching credentials and added me to the UCLA's instructor team. You know how that one went, right, my sparkly head?☆ By taking him all the way to Turkey for an all-expenses-paid trip to be on the stage with me! So together with him, we prepared a very entertaining presentation, where he was explaining the newest trends in marketing and I was evaluating those trends from a customer's point of view according to the psychology of human needs. So I was kinda acting on the stage. ☆ I was sure in my element when I was on the stage, and enjoying speaking about my expectations from the brands as a spoiled customer. 🌟 As I got off the stage, many people lined up in front of me to meet to talk and to take pictures with me! What a wonderful, fulfilling feeling to be recognized as a very motivational motivational speaker! Inter-galactic experience, my Nebula friend! Unexplainable! And one of them was a very different man who had colored-eyes, and very high energy. He gave me his card and with a huge smile on his face he said: "I'm Ozgur Atanur, business development director of Dogan Egmond. I am so impressed with your content, your body language, your tonality and your comfort of being yourself on the stage! As Dogan Publishing, we would like to publish your book." And that's how I got this book published in Turkey, my cosmic, shining and sparkling cosmic friend, my gleaming friend 🌟 And by the way, Dogan Publishing is the biggest and the most prestigious publishing company in Turkey; they are like Hay House of Turkey! So I was extremely honored to receive such an offer from them! 🌟 It immediately put me among A-Class, celebrity authors in my home country, with my first ever book!

But as we all know, life is full of happiness and sadness, my happy star. When I returned to LA at the beginning of May, I immediately called my Anooshjoon and gave him the good news. I said, "Do you remember my book that I started to write two years ago? The biggest publishing house of Turkey will publish it! This weekend I'm going to Las Vegas, but we should meet as soon as I come back. I'll explain to you all the details. I'm so excited." "Of course," he said. "Call me as soon as you come back. I'm waiting." When I came back from Las Vegas, it was Mother's Day and I called him to joke about it. I said. "My dear Anooshjoon, happy Mother's Day!" We laughed and had fun on the phone. I couldn't know that this was also the last phone call I was making with him. His heart stopped that night when he was playing football. :(Just like my dear daddy, he also chose to join the stars in the sky and become light. And at the exact same age as my father, just 57. I was telling him that he was my American dad. I was telling him, "Because I've lost my father, you're my father now. You've opened your heart, your home and your divine soul at the other end of the world and guided me, so therefore you're my second father, Anooshjoon." I wanted to make a movie about him and let the whole humanity know about the existence of such a holy man.

At least with this book, I am able to tell the whole world about him!

Pain is also a part of your galactic journey, my dear cosmic princess. And just like the cosmos, our miraculous life journey will also have an end. The most important thing is to remember that both the pains and joys of this journey are an experience and that it is called "life." And to understand that every experience life gives you is a lesson you need to learn in your cosmic journey. Because with everything you learn you'll first illuminate your thoughts, and then understand that your soul is a stardust made with the same elements of the stars in the sky and by focusing on your goal that awaits you on your orbit, you'll shine with a bright sparkle!!!

My cosmic journey was always about focusing on the target, dear sky princess. Knowing what I didn't want had always brought me closer to what I wanted. When I was very little, I refused to tidy my brother's bed and moved to the next room in the house. My dad bought a house in Ankara because both my brother and I were there as students, but I refused to live in that house and preferred to live on the campus of METU, which was filled with adventures, friendships and experiences that I will carry in my heart for the rest of my life. After that, I again preferred the unknown instead of the "comfortable" life in Ankara and went to Istanbul. It is as if all these things were my spiritual exams on my journey of BEING myself.

I knew very well that I didn't want my given life in Anamur. I knew that I didn't want to work for the government in Ankara as a diplomat. And even when many of my friends had started to work in the finance business with very high salaries, I knew very well that world wasn't my world. I wanted to work in communication, advertising and media. After that, I wanted to be in America. And I wanted to have a work experience in America. After that, I realized the things I couldn't get from advertising and wanted to go to the customer's side. And when I was a customer, I wanted to broaden the vision of the company I was working in, to think globally and create difference. Because at my core, I was listening to my heartbeats in everything I do. I wanted a global vision for my life and to leave a mark that creates difference. All these were not the targets of the companies I worked but my own. They all were not belonging to the brands that I've managed, but my own communication techniques. And again, they all were the truths that I couldn't realize, not the people that I worked with.

Everything I was living was ME. I was the one who was personally choosing everything I was living. And with every target that I had reached, I was a little more in that COSMIC reason.

5 STEPS TO BECOME A GALACTIC LEADER
A STAR IS A GALACTIC LEADER.
BE-LIVE IN U & LET YOUR POWER SHINE OUT!

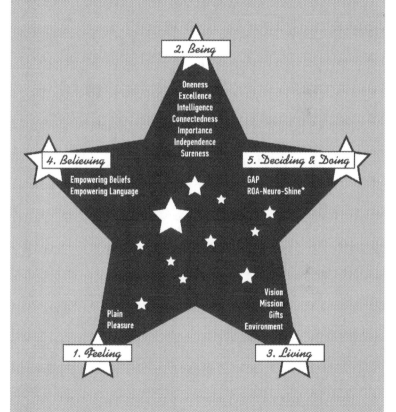

My "Shiny" Results

It's been 20 years since I said that sentence, dear stardust, that *"One day I would live a life like the one I saw in 90210."* And for that I first Be-Live'd and I worked very hard and then success came along. I recreated myself from a little girl from a little town in Turkey into a successful American lady with her new name: SHINY! ⭐And, yes, even though a lot of people think that it's my nickname, it is not, my darling. It is my legal name! I adopted that name as my first name after becoming a citizen. Remember my awakening with Shola? My mission? Well my mission I know now is to make people shine and I now go: *"Hi, my name is Shiny and I make people shine!"* Because I did it to myself! I literally recreated myself as **The Shiny One.** And today, my heart beats for helping people experience this type of a transformation that I have experienced within my soul.

And for this very mission to make people shine, I have been collecting resources and reprogramming my mind with the latest tools, strategies, best practices and technologies that I was learning only from the best in the world! Here is my summary: from 2010 to 2015, I not only received my second bachelor's degree from Metaphysics, my Master's in Metaphysical Psychology and began my PhD, but I also self-educated myself for my second PhD in success studies. Within these five years, I attended over 100 seminars, received over 30 certifications and studied more than 15,000 hours! I did Landmark Forum and Kabbalah classes every week and UCLA Neuroscience Conferences every year. I studied Positive Psychology by Martin Seligman, attended live personal development seminars by Tony Robbins, Dr. Richard Bandler, Chris Howard, Bill Walsh and Adam Markel. I graduated as a Quantum Leap member from New Peaks (which totals about 1,000 hours of mental and emotional education itself), learned from Dr. Daniel Siegel (Neuroscience), Dr. Michio Kaku (Cosmology), Les Brown, Jack Canfield and Brian Tracy. And I was heavily influenced and inspired by Brendon Burchard and Marie Forleo.

As a result, I had the honor of assisting one the history's most influential names as the co-creator of NLP, Dr. Richard Bandler, as one of his assistant NLP trainers in July 2015. I received 9 out of 9 as my Leadership Instructor evaluation score at UCLA Extension from my students, who are professionals working at American Express, Walt Disney, Time Warner Cable, IBM, etc. I personally designed UCLA Extension's first online leadership course. I became dear friends with influential names like Richard Tan and Veronica Tan, the owners of Success Resources, and Michelle Patterson, the CEO of Women Network, who also attended my NLP Training in 2015 together with her beloved husband, Eric. I also met an incredible forward thinker, entrepreneur and a real example of a galactic leader named Chris Kay, who also took my NLP Training in 2015 and later became my corporate client and dear friend.

I made so many people shine both in their personal and professional lives with my training and coaching solutions that I feel gave my life an extra ordinary, galactic meaning today, my stardust. As I said before, I had executive directors from Walt Disney, Verizon and Time Warner Cable, as well as many other international professionals in my Leadership Communication Strategies and Emotional Intelligence courses that I teach at UCLA Extension. I also had the general manager of Turkish Airlines, the

VP of Beverly Hills BMW and several CEOs, real estate brokers, engineers, entrepreneurs, marketing experts, speakers, coaches and trainers in my NLP trainings. I coach very successful entrepreneurs and multi-million dollar business owners today and help them take their life to even higher, galactic levels and shine like real stars up in the cosmic sky!

But my biggest transformation project was my very own cosmic mother, my darling! Yep, my dear mommy.⭐ By applying the powerful, magical and transformational tools of NLP, I literally transformed my mother from an unhappy, victimized, conservative, criticizing 60-year-old woman to an incredibly resourceful, self-reliant, open minded, Shiny and happy 60-year-young galactic leader. ⭐After losing my father right next to her bed in 2006, she never forgave herself until 2013. She was not feeling she "deserved" to have a good time or even laugh because she couldn't help him. She was not feeling "good enough" to live life fully and enjoy herself. She was limiting herself with negative thoughts and feelings and not even wearing any makeup or any jewelery, as they were associated to enjoying life in her mind. Oh, my. She was the toughest case to work on! And that was the year, 2013, I brought her here to LA and worked on her day and night, coaching her, training her, re-programming her mind with healing, liberating and empowering thoughts and activities every single day so that she could start seeing the world with different eyes. In addition to personally educating her about the power of her mind, I also took her to Vegas, to the roller coaster in New York New York hotel and instructed her to leave her fears behind. I made her play the whack-a-mole game in Santa Monica Pier and again instructed her to imagine all those heads popping up as her limiting beliefs and negative voices in her head so that she could associate managing them with her awareness. I took her to San Diego Zoo and made her take the sky-ride with me and she started enjoying the heights.⭐ By the time we were back to Santa Monica to do the Ferris spinning wheel, she was posing for my camera at the top! ⭐ And then she kept coming to my NLP Trainings for the next three years, being one of my best students ever and studying all the principles and techniques all over again.

The result? Well, I am proud to say that today my mom is my Licensed NLP Master Practitioner and Professional Life Coach. She not only transformed herself as an incredibly rescourceful, forward-thinking individual, but she is also working on transforming her community back in my home town by giving seminars and coaching kids and parents on how to think differently and communicate more effectively with the power of NLP! In her recent Women's Day seminar, she had 200 people in the room, even in a very small town like that! I am such a proud daughter for my galactic mother!

So just like my mother, I was able to touch so many more lives and made them shine even brighter in their orbits, my darling.⭐

Here is a list of few success stories on how I made people shine with my training & coaching solutions:

- ✓ Successful entrepreneur (listed on INC500) Chris Kay took my NLP Training and he said I was the best in the world. Watch here: https://www.youtube.com/watch?v=dq9SKUbNv5E
- ✓ My dear Michelle Patterson, the executive producer of California Women's Conferences, took my NLP Training and she said it was the best time she

ever spent together with her husband: https://www.youtube.com/watch?v=5IMXJGMpzoY

✓ I did the branding for my dear friend Hatice Korkmaz's Instagram account and came up with her color theme, her positioning as the "Color Queen" and her slogan "See the world in color," and she went from 390,000 followers to 1.3 million followers after my branding and became an Instagram phenomenon: https://www.instagram.com/kardinalmelon/

✓ I became the official Life Coach sponsor for my dear friend Joyce Giraud's (from Real Housewives of Beverly Hills, 2014) Queen of the Universe beauty pageant in Beverly Hills and did personal branding and coaching for the queens, which I still do every year. http://queenuniversepageant.com/sponsor.html

   ○ I coached Aycan Sencan as Miss Turkey in 2012 and she literally let her cosmic power shine out after that: https://www.instagram.com/aycansencan/

   ○ I coached Ivette Saucedo in 2013 and she also became a galactic leader in her own orbit: https://www.instagram.com/ivettesaucedo/

These are just a few to name, my starlight. You can find more of the Shiny results I helped people create here on my website: https://www.Be-LiveinU.com/

And together in helping these galactic leaders shine came along my own Shiny results. I have appeared on numerous stages; spoken on several international conferences; been interviewed on Turkish National TV, newspapers and magazines several different times; personally trained over 1,000 people; licensed over 100 people as NLP Practitioners and NLP master practitioners all over the world; touched thousands of people's lives; got over 160,000 views on my YouTube channel; created my on-demand online courses at: http://www.Be-LiveinU-training.com/; published this book in January 2016 in Turkey; and got selected as one of 40 UNDER 40 Most Successful Turkish Americans living in America.

So, yes, it's been 20 years since I said that sentence, dear stardust, that *"One day I would live a life like the one I saw in 90210."* And after all these efforts and many ebbs and flows, where I began my journey with $900 in my pocket and a passion to live life fully, cosmically, I'm now living a colorful, meaningful, powerful and very independent life, full of opportunities, on the Shiny streets of Los Angeles with tall palm trees, just like I saw in my show 90210. And it's incredible how I was able to create a shift in my mindset and go from beginning my journey with $900 in my pocket to charging $900 an hour to make people shine and enjoying my SHINY life with six figures today! I'm living with the endless possibilities I've created within the frames I've drawn myself and with the people I've chosen my darling. Now, I'm shining like those cheerful stars I used to watch in the dark sky, and living the dreams I had in that little coastal town! ⭐
AND, YOU CAN DO IT, TOO!

Wondering how?

Well, as you've already witnessed my journey by reading it, sometimes I was in darkness. I encountered hardships and pain but I also experienced desire's resilient resistance, too, my lovely. I have lit a candle on top of that darkness. I took only one step, then lit one more candle, and took one more little step and lit one more candle. With each of them I lived little elevations—little candles that gave little satisfactions with their little lights.

And these little scented candles became a cutely shining, joyfully dancing STAR that is full of life. A holy STAR that had a cosmic power within that takes its light from the darkness. A star that shines brighter with each step. An attractive, fabulous GALACTIC STAR that shines with fabulous lights, exists with its humanly emotions, and dances together in the space with its other galactic companions ...

I became a GALACTIC STAR who first lived her given life, then questioned the unquestioned and created her own comfortable life. And then, when the holy power within her was activated, leaped out of that comfort zone to much greater heights and started to pursue cosmic satisfactions that can be experienced in sky dynamics, my darling. Yes, finally I let my power shine out, baby! And even though this is already a very divine, cosmic joy to experience, I know that I will always be pursuing some other orbits to discover and some other skies that I can shine brighter! ☆

Because I know something very clearly from the times when I was a little girl, when I was just a tiny STARDUST, my darling, that I'M A STAR, A GALACTIC LEADER WHO WAS BORN TO SHINE! Just like you, my stardust. We are stardust and we were born to SHINE!!!

XOXO, The Shiny One ☆

It is in the moments of your crystal clear, soul-felt and electrifying decisions that you shine your galactic path!

~ *SHINY BURCU UNSAL*

"How to Be-Live in U"

Dear Shiny,

First of all, congratulations for making the decision to absolutely Be-Live in U and let your divinely touched and infinitely blessed inner power shine out, my darling! What a superstar attitude to begin your galactic success path! And what a fantastic way to rock your soul and honor your being! I am so excited for you, my darling!

Second, as you really want to let your beautiful soul power shine out into your moments, your days and eventually into your whole galactic path, you are gonna have to make a big fat committed decision and act upon it right away, my galactic friend! That's the whole point of holding this magical book in your skillful hands: getting to know that powerful galactic leader waiting inside of your soul; showing her how to come out in the most fascinating, magnificent way possible to rock your world; and letting it shine out like the most breath-taking cosmic jewelry ever!

Because, darling, it's in those moments of your big, heartfelt, committed decisions that you can cosmically shine your galactic path. And a big, committed decision inside of you needs a big, committed action outside of you in order to grow out of you and shine your days through! ⭐ Plus, any earthy creature can claim that she is a good decision maker, but we all know that a great decision maker is the one who can prove her superstar galactic decision with a real, promising galactic action.

Hence, I am inviting you to be the best decision maker you have ever consciously been and make the biggest, the juiciest and the shiniest decision that you have ever made in your entire galactic being, my darling. Your decisions are the most important moments into getting what you want and shining your path along. And in order to master your decision making skills, I will take you through a very comprehensive decision making process that you will really enjoy, my dear. And this process will come with understanding your feelings, measuring your galactic needs, having your cosmic mission and vision cleared out, really deeply believing in yourself and the path you are choosing; and then of course, doing whatever it cosmically takes to let your galactic power shine out! This's all it takes for you to finally make that big, fat, juicy decision with your entire being, my darling. ☆

And along the way, I'll share some really profound cosmic laws, some basic galactic rules and some other universal principles that govern our universe that you can use as tools when you are going through each and every step toward that big spiritual decision of yours darling.

But before I share them, let me make some really important distinctions about the vocabulary I am using here, my lovely Shiny:

First of all, I am calling you "Shiny" because my whole goal here is to make you shine so bright like you have never done before. ☆ So to me, you are already glowing since you picked this book to let your power shine out! I am honoring your dedication by calling you "Shiny"! Plus, I feel really connected to the light of our Universal Creator, when I use the vocabulary of light, like Shiny, glory, glowing, dazzling, mesmerizing and all that.

Oh, I am also calling you my darling, my dear, my sweetheart, sweetie, dearest, sparky and all that as well to keep your heart close to mine, darling! Can you feel it? ☆ ☆ ☆ Feel me in your heart, darling! Feel the beat of my heart, smiling to you in these lines. ⭐ Yes, I'm smiling and you are feeling it. ⭐

OK, now we can move on to the cosmology part of my language.

Cosmically speaking, there are three types of beings in our universe, according to the level of their consciousness. The first one is the lowest level being that I call as "physical beings," the second one is the one in the middle and that's why I call them "transit beings," and finally the top one is the highest level of being that I call "**galactic beings.**"

Physical beings are almost like robotic machines that are experiencing everything only through their physical bodies—missing out everything mystical, metaphysical and cosmic—because they are not able to tap into their spiritual power within. And that in itself is causing them to have a lower level of consciousness and being mostly in a "reactive" mood throughout their existence. These human beings are almost disconnected from the force of light and the divine love of the universe, because they are stuck in the 10-percent realities of their physical world. Focusing on the pain, feeling sorry for themselves, being reactive towards life and others, living as a victim and blaming anything but their own decisions, and believing in mere coincidences of life rather than the cause and effect are some common practices of these physical beings.

They are trapped in their unconscious patterns of victim mentality, leaving no room for true meaning of charge, juice or joy in their life. Physical beings live a type of life that I call the "**given**" life, far from being consciously designed or proactively created, but very much about reactively experienced, which I will further explain in the upcoming chapters. And so, they live a half-life, an obedient and a pre-shaped destiny which is a mere projection of other beings' wishes, demands and desires from what to eat to how to sit to what to say to how to say it. Far, far, far away from being of Galactic nature, far, far away from the light of the universe, away from their cosmic power within.

There are only two ways out of this "given," "pre-exposed" and "reactive" life, my darling: either something new will come into your life and wake you up from your sleep and raise you up from your ashes, or something new will come out of you and let your cosmic power shine out through you!

Even though I have always been against the conservative rituals, old-school thinking, traditional norms and unquestioned forms of our given lives where there is an insane amount of social hypnosis going on, I must confess that I have had my own share of the "reactive" moments, felt my own way of the repressions and been in my own mental imprisonment of the controlled, pre-determined, judgmental and hypnotized structure of the given life. To be honest, it did not feel good at all. It literally sucked! I felt trapped, like a cute little mouse chasing after the instant gratifications of a piece of cheese here and a piece of cheese there, having no over-lasting taste on the tongue of my life! It was all temporary. It was all trying to get by, among the given choices that the given life has given to me, placing me in the midst of the physical beings, without my noticing that low-conscious, powerless and always-complaining version living very inside of me!

I may not have been able to break free of the given life, because here is the sobering part: Some will never will. But I did, because something new came out of me through the ENLIGHTENMENT I had from reading tons of self-help books and watching self-help movies, like the legendary movie The Secret.🌟 Yes, I was enlightened and I did break free, only to realize that I have become a

<u>transit passenger</u> on my way up to the galactic lights of the cosmic life.

YOU ARE A STAR!
BE PROACTIVE
NOT REACTIVE

Transit beings are the ones who are living what I call a "**comfortable**" life. It's hard for them to give up this comfort even though they knew that they are not living up to their real, cosmic potential inside since they worked so hard to create this comfortable life with some trade-offs they had to make, a few more hours at the office here, a little less freedom there. When we are here at this comfort level, we are not living our truth, and not being our powerful, independent and totally "alive" galactic versions. Through hard work, commitment, other beings around us or simply pure galactic power (luck) we have been able to break free of the social hypnosis that was imposed on us because we were better off financially, emotionally and socially. Or have we really?

As transit beings, we feel comfortable in this way until one day someone asks, "How is life?" and we respond, "Could have been better." Sound familiar? And then we start wondering, *"Is this really what I wanted? Am I living a life worth living or are there any other possibilities I can still explore? What if there is more in life? There must be something more! I feel like I am not tapping into my full potential. But do I have the courage to go after it? Can I leave everything behind? Everything I have worked so hard for to build? I am so comfortable where I am right now, is it really worth the trouble chasing after a place called unknown? Oh, Gosh. I don't know! I cannot decide!!!"* Sound familiar?

Been there and done that, as well. This is the level where you really need to feel the calling of the universe from the core of your being and let the transformation take over control rather than you trying too hard to be in control, in vain. You are never in control anyways. We think and want to Be-Live that we are, but are we really? Or is that power coming from an infinite source of energy that we all are a part of? Yes, we do have the free will, the choices, and our heartfelt decisions to make. But is it really being in control, being able to make your own decisions? Did you ever think about it? If you haven't, it might be your time to look at the bigger picture and start to see the secrets of our magnificent existence.

Life doesn't have to be unknown, mysterious or meaningless like we feel here at the transit level. Your soul doesn't have to feel incomplete and decisions don't have to be hard to make like a transit being experiences at this level. Yes, there is more to life and, yes, we can experience a whole new version of ourselves when we rise up to the heights of the Shiny fancy galactic stars in the sky! If only we can break free of our FEARs to meet the incredible, cosmic, galactic versions of ourselves on the other side of our fears!

And we all know what it takes: A big, fat, heart-felt and committed decision to BE and LIVE in the best version of our selves! A little EMPOWERMENT!

Galactic beings on the other hand, are the real spiritual beings in their physical bodies, living a joyfully fulfilled **cosmic life**, with a higher level of consciousness of this magnificent universe, having access to the 90-percent spiritual reality of our cosmic structure. They Be-Live in their intuitive feelings, they speak the universal language of unconditional love, and they live in a higher level of wisdom where everything happens for a reason,. There is always a spiritual learning in what seems to be the pain, as well as being in the cosmic mood and living the miracles each and every breath that they take in. They are the visionary and the creator people with a flexible and a free mind that can go up and down alongside the global information that are entered into their cosmic brains. They love to step up and rise up, and they have no apologies for being in touch with their awesome, shining and motivating cosmic power within!

And YOU—my dear SHINY—you happen to be the greatest version of your **galactic being** because you are a galactic leader, darling!

Galactic leaders are elevated beings who feel responsible for their decisions, actions and relations along their path and whatever they do. They search for becoming ONE with the universe, because they know that they are already a part of ONE BIG SHINY UNIVERSE.

☆Similarly, since they have a divine connection with the creator of the universe, they understand the language of the universe very well. And they write, speak and listen to the language of the universe. They can even read its signs and integrate the whole dynamics of human excellence into one single cosmic message that they receive from the creator:

Be-Live in U!

YOU ARE A STAR!

Let's break down the cosmic message of the universe to its components:

1. **Be you**: Because everybody else is already taken! ☆And you can only Become U, the different versions of U, and hopefully the best version. ☆
2. **Live you**: Because you can only live your own life in your own physical body and feel what's inside your body, like every other living being.
3. **Believe in you**: Because you will achieve greatness only if you believe in you!
4. **Be LIVE in you**: Because only after discovering your own magnificent being and your miraculous living, can you be alive and feel complete and **live** within you.

So the cosmic message of a galactic leader is: **Be-Live in U**. Be the leader in U so that you can let your inner galactic power shine out!

What does it mean?

Well, when you let your power shine out, you can be who you are meant to be. And when you become who you are meant to be, then you can do what your soul wants to do. When you can do what your souls wants to do, then you can really live the way your soul yearns to live. And when you can experience the new you with your new beliefs and with your new behaviors, then you can have all you want to have. All you want to have, with your body, with your mind and with your soul. So it's actually a secret, obviously, a galactic formula, that I collected from the moons and the stars and the galaxies for you.☆ It will teach you how to get real results in life. It's your recipe to bake your superstar cake, with the right amount of ingredients, in the right order with the right purposes.

Think about it, Shiny. Your soul wants to experience life through your being, so it wants you to BE. And your mind exists so that you can DO whatever it's created to do. Eventually giving your physical body whatever it wants to HAVE. So, first you are going to BE and DO and finally HAVE whatever you want to BE-DO-HAVE. And that's what we are going to call your shining success path as a galactic leader as your cosmic formula to "**Be-Live in U**."

BE - DO- HAVE

YOU ARE A STAR!
BE-LIVE IN U

Be-Live in U is what this little Shiny book is all about, darling. You are here with me, now, about to take on a new, exciting, promising and fascinating journey to learn and practice how to Be-Live in U as an amazing galactic leader and let your cosmic power shine out!

And since you are interested in what the universe has to say for you, you do have a big responsibility, darling. Because galactic leaders are the only cosmic beings that can elevate the consciousness of our galactic era, translate the language of the universe to other human beings and help the whole humanity move forward!

So, are you ready to take on this cosmic challenge and serve the whole humanity, my darling? If YES, then let's start with 10 Cosmic Laws that every galactic leader needs to know about the universe that we live in:

YOU ARE A STAR!
SERVE
HUMANITY

10 Cosmic Laws of the Universe
For You to Be-Live in U

1. THE LAW OF DIVINE ONENESS: You are literally made of stardust.

This very first cosmic law states that we live in a universe where everything is connected to everything else. And everything together forms the one, big, gigantic universal oneness. So everything we say, we do, we Be-Live and we have affects others. Because we are one, from a cosmic perspective. And this divine oneness is the very core principle of our galactic existence. Everything—the sun and the moon and the galaxies, stars, galactic leaders, human beings, feelings, thoughts, motions, etc.—we are all one, vibrating with a certain rhythm of universal energy.

The carbon, nitrogen and oxygen atoms consciously co-existing together with the atoms of other heavy elements created in previous generations of stars over 4.5 billion years ago, just to form the perfect structure of your human body, is what you are made of. So, at its deep core, a very conscious, cosmically governed starfdust is what your human body is made up of. Just like galaxies are made up of self-conscious planets and stars, coming together in perfect harmony and co-existing for billions of years, to form a bigger system of light. So, everything is conscious energy in the universe; including our physical bodies. Start with your own body. Your physical machine is more magnificent than you can ever imagine. Did you know that there are about 100 trillion cells in your body? Let me say it again: 100 trillion cells! Do you know what that means? Since there are about 400 billion galaxies in the universe, it means that the number of the cells in your human body is about 2,500 times bigger than the number of the galaxies in the whole universe! And by the time you read this sentence you will have already lost 300 million cells in your body. But don't worry. ⭐ Because, you will be producing 300 billion more cells today! That's how cosmically intelligent, how fascinating, magnificent and mind blowing divine conscious is that you have inside of you!

That's why you need your cosmic energy flowing in your divine oneness. Which means you need an earthy INTEGRITY in what you say and what you do, honey! That's exactly what makes you a cosmic superstar, with your divine cosmic power within!

2. THE LAW OF POLARITY: Pain only exists for you to appreciate the pleasure.

Everything is on a continuum and has an opposite in the universe, even the universe itself. The galaxies of the universe keep shining because there is dark matter making their lights so bright and so visible. There are days and there are nights. There are negative elements and there are positive elements. There is pain and there is pleasure.

So, PAIN came as only a different type of experience for human beings to comprehend and learn from. The aim was to elevate the human being. So that they could GAIN from their PAIN. It's also good to remember that no rainbow came before a little rain. ⭐ Because, at the beginning, there was only **LIGHT**. Before the physical world, there was only the spiritual world. Where LIGHT only knew to give and share. But the human being wanted to earn what he was receiving so he asked for a challenge. Only overcoming a challenge the light would be earned and deserved in the dark matter of human space. And so humanity received the PAIN from the light, in addition to the infinite pleasure of their ever-existing being.

So, yes, my darling, you can suppress and transform your undesirable thoughts by concentrating on the opposite pole with your earthy habit of POSITIVE THINKING and it is a cosmic princess' job to do that! ⭐

3. THE LAW OF CORRESPONDENCE: Our physical world represents only 1 percent.

This law states that the principles or laws of physics that explain the physical world—energy, light, vibration and motion—have their corresponding principles in the etheric, or the universe. "As above, so below...."

So, what you see as reality is not really the reality, my cosmic princess.⭐ It's the perception of your reality. And it only represents the 1 percent of the universal, the cosmic reality. It seems like there is a huge 99 percent left out of what we live in, as the spiritual realm of our cosmic experience. It seems like that because we are here on this planet earth, to experience the realm of physicality with our physically limited bodies. Is it really the case, though? Not really! Because we already are from the realm of spirituality and we already know all we need to know! So we are not these physical beings who are here to experience the realm of spirituality; we are here as these miraculous spiritual beings, who are here to experience the realm of physicality. And that 99-percent realm of spirituality will only be remembered through your human being experiences of your physical life, as you already have that cosmic knowing of 99 percent bulit inside of you! Very mind-blowing when you re-read and think about it, right, my stardust?

So your job as a cosmic stardust, my darling, is to remain connected to the realm of your spirituality and **STAY IN THE KNOWING** in your physical experience so that you can get the most fascinating physical experiences in your galactic journey!

4. THE LAW OF CAUSE AND EFFECT: Everything happens for a bigger, cosmic reason:

There is cosmic intelligence governing the whole structure of the universe, from earth to oceans, from seasons to climates, from feelings to physical happenings. And so, everything happens for a cosmic reason. For every action there is a reaction. Nothing happens outside of the universal laws. Even the things that don't happen, they don't happen for a reason. A reason that you may not enjoy or find extremely unpleasant at the time being, but absolutely creates miracles in a bigger, cosmic picture of the universe. And in order to see the bigger picture, you need to rise above the physical illusions of your reality, climb over the clouds, pass the moon and reach out to the Shiny stars. And then look down again, my Shiny darling, only to see how small your challenge is compared to the cosmic reason you see from the top and to the power of the superstar that you can really be.

So your job is to **GET A UNIVERSAL PERSPECTIVE** by raising your consciousness above and beyond your physical reality to remember to trust your struggle—because there is a cosmic reason behind everything that's happening in your journey.

5. THE LAW OF VIBRATION: The more the gratitude, the happier your life is.

Gratitude is one of the highest levels of cosmic vibrations we can ever feel as spiritual beings, my darling. And it is the level of vibration that our souls yearn to radiate infinitely. It's the secret of the cosmic world implanted in the DNAs of galaxies, planets, moons and stars. Look at the sky and you will see the infinite harmony of the billions of galaxies above, radiating gratitude and stillness with a perfect meaning of the universe. Look at your life and you will see the best moments that you always remember are the moments when you feel happy and alive and when you are aware that you are happy and alive. Gratitude is accepting and being aware that your existence (feeling alive) is already the meaning of your life. And this is a sacred duty of a cosmic princess, my dear.

When you feel grateful, you are sending universe a cosmic message that your very stardust nature inside is aligned with your galactic journey you are living outside. And that alone is the most powerful vibration to practice the law of attraction in your earthy experience, my dear cosmic princess! If you can manage to vibrate at this high level of energy day in and day out, you will attract the most magnificent people, situations and feelings to your Shiny galactic path!

So your job is to practice more **GRATITUDE** every day so that you can attract more things you can be grateful for along the way.

6. THE LAW OF RHYTHM: Your mind is your ultimate communication tool between your body and your soul.

This law states that everything vibrates and moves with a certain rhythm, the rhythm of the universe. And your existence, my gorgeous Stardust, your soul, being a cosmic light at its core, does vibrate with this universal rhythm, including your mind, your body and your soul. And your mind is your only tool to connect your physical body and your spirit, your soul. The key here, my darling, is your ability to tune in to the rhythm of the universe, to get the most important information in its best practical form. So let's take a look at your being and how to connect the three pillars of your being to each other by vibrating with the rhythm of the universe.

There are three components of every living being: **Body-Mind-Soul**. The first component is the essence of life, the force of life, the soul, or the spirit. Your soul is your connection to the realm of the spiritual reality and therefore it always searches to become ONE with the universe. It's already one with the universe; it's a part of it. Your soul is all about the Light at its core. And your soul speaks the universal language of Love & Light, because it has the wisdom of the cosmic intelligence from billions of years of existence.

The second component of your being is your eternally powerful mind. Your mind is your only tool to communicate between your body and your soul. It translates the language of your soul (feelings) as emotions in your physical body and filters all of your nerve impulses generated by your body, including your emotions, as your experiences in your physical world. The quality of the communication between your soul and your mind, and the quality of the communication between your body and your mind depends totally on your ability to use your mind effectively. When the mind is used effectively, it is at its peak creativity and productivity because it's quiet, focused and conscious. Your mind is your only tool to create the bridge of your magnificent life between your body and your soul. So your job is to quiet your mind and make it focus on the results you set for yourself, so that it can collect the right kind of knowledge and the wisdom from the soul and apply it in your body.

The third part of your being is your body. Your physical body, unlike your mind and your soul, is a mortal machine limited with time and space. It is your physical packaging on the outside, and it is the by-product of the communication between your mind and your soul. Your body operates miraculously with the cosmic intelligence received from the wisdom of the soul and manages about 75 billion to 100 billion cells without needing your mind's conscious attention. Your heart never forgets to beat, your organs are all run by themselves, and your neurons communicate and interact by themselves, so your internal body is already self-conscious. In summary, almost 95 percent of your entire phsycial machine is self-conscious, not needing your awareness. Think about it, Shiny. Ninety-five percent!!! So all you have left to consciously decide is only the remaining 5 percent, which is understanding and managing your conscious mind to establish the smoothest communication between your body and your soul.

Overall, these three components of your galactic being need to co-exist in harmony, the harmony of the universal rhythm. The universal rhythm is the rhythm of action. It is the rhythm of love, the rhythm of wisdom and universal service. So once you have that deep understanding of universal service, you will naturally find a way to do all that it takes to catch the rhythm of life, my shiniest treasure. And you will already know how to create that cosmic harmony by acting according to the laws of the universe.

Therefore, your job as a cosmic princess is first to maintain the health of your living shell by applying a healthy balanced eat-sleep-exercise-generate-energy lifestyle and then to connect your mind to the **UNIVERSAL SERVICE** in whatever decision, action and any kind of passion you are going to own, my darling. That's all.

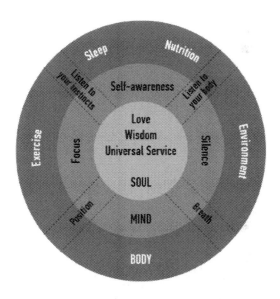

7. THE LAW OF ATTRACTION: What goes around comes back around.

Nothing happens suddenly in our world. There is always a cause and always an effect, my stardust darling. And whatever the cause you seed in become the results you take in. So your first job here about this cosmic law is to take responsibility of your actions, inactions, behaviors, misbehaviors, communications and miscommunications, darling. Your job, like the moons and the stars and the billions of other galaxies of the universe, is to become a galactic leader, so that you can make better decisions and take better actions collectively, to help our humanity move forward. Because, all 7 billion of us here on this planet today, are just like those 400 billion galaxies of the universe, a part of a bigger cause. The bigger the cause the bigger the responsibility. So as a galactic leader of a big, universal cause, it is your personal responsibility to calculate the results of your actions before you take them as your lovely beloved decisions. Because whatever you think about, you'll talk about. And whatever you talk about, you'll feel about. And eventually whatever you feel about, you will bring about. You cannot fill your mind with darkness and negativity and expect to have a bright, positive life around you, darling! You know that. What goes around will come back around!

So your second job in here is to **PAUSE and THINK: "WHERE IS MY CONSCIOUSNESS THAT I AM ATTRACTING BACK TO MY MAGNETIC GALACTIC PATH?"** before you take any of your decisions and your actions, my glowing kind of stardust. ☆

YOU ARE A STAR!
THOUGHTS BECOME THINGS

8. THE LAW OF ACTION: Your biggest power is your ability to Be-Live in U and take action.

Action means decision. Decision means idea. Idea means focus. Focus means desire. And desire means soul. Your desires are your biggest powers, residing inside of your soul! And you have the power to tap into your soul's deepest desires and let your cosmic power shine out with glitters, my cosmic princess!

When you look at the history of the universe, you will understand that everything started with taking action, with the Big Bang. The elements, the stars, the planets, the galaxies and then the love and pain and the trees and the flowers and even we, the human beings, all emerged from the very first action of the Light. So it is in our very core that we are born to take action and create things, my darling. Creation lies within the moments of cosmic actions. Creation takes place if and only there is action. And that action has to be forced by a big, fat commitment—a cosmic decision. We call the process of making that cosmic decision your ability to Be-Live in U as a Shiny glamourous and gorgeous galactic leader with your cosmic power inside of you, my dear.

So your job as a Shiny galactic leader made up of stardust is to **TAKE AND TAKE AND TAKE ACTION UNTIL IT MAKES YOU SHINE** (gets you want you want) in your earthy journey and never ever give up, my cosmic darling!

9. THE LAW OF RELATIVITY: We are here to experience BEING, not doing or having.

This law states that every being will receive a series of tests to go through during his or her life here in the physical world for the purpose of strengthening the Light within. These tests show up in life as problems, and these problems are not at all the stop signs, but rather they are your guidelines to your cosmic shine within, darling. You must consider each of these tests to be a challenge and remain connected to your heart when proceeding to solve your problems. Your heart is where you are connected to your soul. Therefore, remaining connected to your soul will remind you of the wisdom and give you the strength to carry on, my galactic princess. ⭐

This law also teaches us the subjectivity and the relativity of our problems compared to each other's problems so that we can put everything into its proper perspective. No matter how bad we perceive our situation to be, there can always be someone who feels he or she is in a worse position. It is all relative. So your purpose here is to BECOME who you are born to BE, through doing and having things, by understanding the rhythm of the universe, rising above the negative cycles and patterns in your life, while remaining connected to your heart and to your universal service.

The cosmos exists with billions of galaxies for billions of years. And if we are to model the structure of the universe, we see the shining light of its galaxies regardless of the 70 percent of the dark matter that also exists throughout the billions of years of the cosmic life. It is the same for us as beings. Complaining about the challenges you face throughout your galactic journey will provide no benefit and makes no sense because you will know that somebody else with less resources and bigger challenges somewhere in this planet is achieving to Be-Live in his or her power somehow and hence brightly shining!

So your job as a cosmic princess is to BE a shining LIGHT, which means **MAINTAIN YOUR FOCUS ON THE SOLUTIONS RATHER THAN THE PROBLEMS**, regardless of the darkness you experience throughout the years of your cosmic existence, my stardust darling.

10. THE LAW OF PERPETUAL TRANSMUTATION OF ENERGY: Dedication and commitment is the secret for a cosmically fulfilling life.

That's what it takes to lead a galactic superstar life my stardust. Think about chemical elements, and the absolute law of commitment in the chemical world. Salt, for example. What is it made of? Sodium and Chloride: NaCl. For how long? For ever as we know it. What is their secret? Sticking to each other forever and ever. What if they decide to break up and give up on forming salt for us? What happens then? Chaos. Both chemical and existential chaos. Why? Because it's against the cosmic laws of the universe. Well then, how come Sodium and Chloride can decide, take action and commit to serving a greater service, and human beings can't? You are obviously here to practice a dedication and commitment at the highest level of your cosmic existence, darling!

So your job is to **COMMIT TO YOUR COSMIC BEING** simply by practicing *integrity, positive thinking, staying in the knowing, having a universal perspective about your life, practicing gratitude, providing universal service, pausing and thinking where your consciousness is before taking your decisions and actions, taking actions until it gets you what you want, and focusing on the solutions instead of problems,* my galactic gorgeous. ⭐

This is it: Commit! And just do it again and again and again, darling. Because in addition to all these **cosmic laws**, there is also another law, the law of use, which dictates, *"Whatever you don't use, you'll lose,"* my darling. Which takes its root from another law, the law of familiarity that "if you are around anything long enough, you take it for granted." So, don't you dare to take yourself for granted, honey! If you don't wanna lose your identity, you gotta practice your own fidelity. ⭐

YOU ARE A STAR!
ESCALATE
COMMITMENT

So now, Shiny, let's do an exercise about where you are with applying these universal laws as a galactic leader. Just grab a pen a paper—better yet, your galactic notebook—and answer these questions by staying connected to your heart, please. ⭐

1. Remember a time when you were really present in the moment with your whole being, maybe staring at a beautiful flower, playing with a cute little puppy or melting in the eyes of your lover? Just remember how eternal that moment felt, connecting a deeper part of you to that moment, to that person, to that thing or to that experience. How did it feel different from any other moment in your life? What was it that made you connect to that moment with your whole being? How do you explain that?

- -
- -
- -
- -

2. Write down a time when everything seemed very negative and you felt very weak and fearful, but the whole situation turned out to be a total blessing later in your life.

- -
- -
- -
- -

3. Think of a time when you had access to something greater than your everyday intelligence, something beyond your logical mind, and write down the aspect of this deep connection you experienced in your life. How was it? How exactly did you feel?

----

4. Think of a time when you acted upon a
    powerful calling from your heart—even
    though you had no idea what you were
    supposed to do or how you were supposed
    to do it—but somehow you found a way to
    manage it because you really, deeply wanted it
    from your soul. What do you think happened?
    How did you feel? How do you explain it?

----

5. How do you understand when you have your
    "gratitude" mood on? Do you sense a different
    level of peacefulness inside? What happens to
    your thought process when you are in this
    mood, compared to any other moods that you
    have?

----

6. Why do you think there is a specific rhythm
    of our hearts? Do you think that every living
    thing can have its own rhythm of life? How

about your life? What is your everyday
rhythm like? Upbeat? Smooth jazz? Rock'n
Roll? Hip hop? Lounge? House music? Or
maybe Buddha bar?

----

7. Think of a time when you thought about,
   talked about and felt about a dream you had.
   How did it feel to talk about an ideal version
   of you? Did your feelings magnify since you
   were sharing them with others? Now think of
   a time when you only thought about, talked
   about and felt about a problem you had. How
   did that feel to talk about? Did your negative
   feelings also magnify since you were sharing
   them with others? Do you now see clearly
   that what goes around comes back around,
   including your own thoughts and language?
   And do you now also see why you need to
   think positively and talk positively in life?
   Please write down what is your new decision
   about your thoughts.

----

8. Write down what you are afraid of in general.
   The fears that you have, or any source of

pain for you, currently. Also write down the FEARs you used to have and you do not have anymore. What do you think has changed in time? Did something "new" come into your life? Or did something "new" come out of you, about them? What action do you think you took with your cosmic power within that changed the name of your game?

- -
- -
- -
- -

9. Think of a problem or challenge you went through in life that really made you say, "Life is tough." How were you doing at that time compared to six years prior to that time? How many people in the world do you honestly think would swap places with you just to have what you have, even if it comes with the challenges you were experiencing? Would you swap places with someone who just had a major car accident and broke his bones terribly? Write down your answers below, by reminding yourself the power of law of relativity that you can use every time you face a challenge in life.

- -
- -
- -
- -

10. Think of a goal you set for yourself that you really stayed committed to until you got the results you wanted. How was that experience different from all the others? What made you "stick" to it until the end while you dropped all the others during the process?

- -
- -
- -
- -

11. Think of a decision you made or a skill you learned but did not use it or practice it, like learning to play guitar or speaking a language. What was the result? Did you lose your skill because you didn't use it? Did you also lose sight of the decision because you did not pay conscious attention to it?

- -
- -
- -
- -

12. Now think of something or even somebody that you are familiar with—maybe an idea, a technique or even a close friend or your partner you think you know. Is it possible that you take that person or the idea for granted and you are causing yourself to not to get curious about it, not wanting to explore its different dynamics anymore?

----

13. **Last, but not least, now that you have the knowledge and clarity about all these cosmic laws and how you can apply them in your Shiny galactic path, what are some decisions and action steps you can take today?**

How are your answers, my cosmic beauty? Do you recognize the universal clock ticking in your everyday life happenings? Isn't it mind-blowing to realize the pre-framed galactic game we are all playing? Nothing in this gigantic playground remains chaotic. Even the chaos has its own contextual reasoning to exist. Why do you think we created law, religion, governments, states, cities, organizations, clubs, associations, groups or families as human beings? Why do you think there is "language" to start with? How about the reason of the existence of "math" or "chemistry" or, better yet, "neuro science"? Don't you see that the world we live in has a system and within that system we created sub-systems only to imitate and trying to figure out the big, real, factual system?

What do we really have in hand? We have the sun, the moon, the stars, the planets, the galaxies and the dark matter we can all see. We have the oceans, the rivers, the forests, the mother earth with her mountains and stones and sands, and the blue sky with its own routine climate air that repeats itself four times a year but always contains oxygen. We have other living species like animals, plants, flowers, vegetables, natural foods and other living organisms like bacteria. And then we have the time and space and our incredible DNA's with billions of years of information embedded in our individual physical bodies that separate us, as human beings, from one another.

We did not really have any language at the beginning; the first human beings communicated through drawings of what they saw in the nature. Ironically, they did the drawings not to communicate about the object in the drawing, but rather to communicate what that object in the drawing "meant" for them! For example, they drew a picture of a bird in order to communicate the verb of "flying" amongst each other, not to communicate about the bird itself. Simply, they wanted to comprehend the nature visually and also communicate it with others visually. Approximately 70 percent of learning tends to be based on vision. No wonder why we started all visual. We simply modelled the system, the universe we saw around us, and put it in images to create meanings, and then we followed the language.

Same with math and chemistry. First we observed what's around us as our natural system and then we created our own systems to calculate the existing system. Then we created a mathematical/chemical language made up of numbers and formulae.

And now we are in the era of neuroscience, which is more into the realm of the unseen—the non-visual but fortunately scientifically enabled to be seen. Until about 30 years ago, human beings did not know what was inside the brain, literally. But today we know that our neurons are electrically excitable and that their activity predictably affects the electrical state of adjacent neurons. Here is a direct reference from Wikipedia on this fact:

"Decades of research have now shown that substantial changes occur in the lowest neocortical processing areas, and that these changes can profoundly alter the pattern of neuronal activation in response to experience. Neuroscientific research indicates that experience can actually change both the brain's physical structure (anatomy) and functional organization (physiology). Which can be found in the saying of "neurons that fire together wire together"/"neurons that fire apart wire apart," summarizing Hebbian theory: If there are two nearby neurons that often produce an impulse simultaneously, their cortical maps may become one. This idea also works in the opposite way, i.e. that neurons which do not regularly produce simultaneous impulses will form different maps." http://en.wikipedia.org/wiki/Neuroplasticity

I am more on the *"neurons that fire together wire together"* part now. Doesn't it ring a bell about our infinite efforts to imitate the universal system around us? Look at the sun and the moon within the same proximity, firing up together all the time, producing the day and night for us human beings all the time, or the Sodium and Chloride firing up together and wiring up together as salt for us human beings! It's everywhere around you, my cosmic baby, but since we are also wired so perfectly not to "see" the big picture around us, this cosmic system requires an immense amount of focus from all of us as human beings. The real system—the universal structure and the context of our cosmos—reveals itself in our everyday experiences, in our everyday actions and interactions to the one who really wants to and who is also ready to see it.

So wake up, my galactic leader! Wake up to see the cosmic structure around you, which also lies within you. Our cosmos has the same gigantic contextual intelligence in its all larger, smaller and micro systems with the same cosmic laws applied respectively. So wake up to your galactic game, my shining star! Let's get up and let's play! There is so, so, so much to say!

YOU ARE A STAR!
IT'S TIME TO
WAKE UP

Now, darling, let's go through the cosmic laws of the universe once again, and let me share how I used these laws in my galactic journey, so that you can start your shining galactic path with a first-hand shining galactic guideline that can keep you away from the darkness of the unknown.

How I Applied 10 Cosmic Laws of the Universe For Me to Be-Live in Me

1. The law of divine oneness.

Well, my darling, I always felt that I was part of something big and I actually wanted to be a part of something really big. Probably that's why I have always wanted to live in bigger places than my cute little hometown since I was a little girl. So in everything I did, I always followed my heart, chasing that historic feeling of "divine oneness" that made me feel WHOLE and ALIVE. I may not have done this consciously but I felt as if I had this "oneness" core built in my DNA. I became conscious about it during a *value-solicitation exercise* in my NLP trainings in Los Angeles. Before this, I didn't even know that I didn't know about it, my Shiny princess. Can you Be-Live that? Whereas now, I cannot live without it. Today, I still have that "oneness" perspective in my life. I have it as my highest value, above and beyond everything, taking my decisions and actions so as to have that wholeness, oneness darling. For that, I am a galactic being with **integrity**. My talks and my walks are aligned. I keep my promises both to myself and to the physical world around me. Most importantly, I lead a life with a rare understanding in that I Be-Live all belong to a life of a cosmic nature, my darling.

2. The law of polarity.

You know, Shiny, up until now, I went through my own kind of pain and suffering along my path, but I trusted my struggle because I was the one choosing it, wanting to shine from it. And, by the way, I loved overcoming challenges! Trust me; the more you do it, the better you get at it. ⭐So, with every obstacle I have overcome, I feel I have grown stronger and I have become a little wiser. For example, when I had to work so many jobs when I was studying at UCLA Extension, I always focused on the fact that I was doing all that for a temporary period of time. Or again, when I decided to go back to LA in 2010, instead of focusing on how hard it was going to be, I thought about how exciting and fascinating it was going to be. So I chose to see the light in every dark corner, practicing a good dose of **positive thinking** in my life, baby!⭐

3. The law of correspondence.

I Be-Live we are all here to BE what we are choosing to BE, my Shiny little stardust. And for that, the spiritual nature of us cannot—should not—be ignored. You know sometimes you "feel" like doing something extraordinary, something "different" from other people. But the resistance you face from others around you can just take you and break you off that move. Sound familiar, honey? Well, right in those moments, I did what my heart told me to do, not what others told me I should do. I felt like I was **in the knowing** zone of my spirituality. And I felt like the universe was speaking to me through my heartbeats, through my feelings. So I listened to the whispers of the cosmos, darling. I increased the volume of the universe within me instead of the clutter around my physical reality. Just like choosing to be in communication in Istanbul rather than working for the government in Ankara, or just like quitting one job after another job because my being was not satisfied. In every single move of mine, I might

87

have been getting farther away from the people around me but I was totally getting closer to the truth of my spiritual cosmicality. Yes, it felt right, but not at all easy, baby.

4. The law of cause and effect.

This one is really a good one, darling! It's a tenet in the personal development and spiritual thinking world: Everything happens for a reason!!! And, yes, everything did happen for a bigger reason that I did not know in advance darling. I was just to live and learn it that way. For example, if I had never met my dear Anoohjoon, I would have never got my eyes opened to the many blind spots I had in me and so I could have never become who I am today. Or if I had never taken a decision to switch from working in advertising agencies to be an advertiser in my last corporate job, I would have never met that consultant who also opened my eyes to so many other parts of me and who also paved the way for my Harvard Education! Seriously, look at your life, Shiny, and tell me for what purpose situations and people came in to your life by just tracing back in time, darling. Don't you see the master plan we are in? So, just by realizing this very truth of my life, I have been leading my life, at least for the last five years, with this amazingly calming universal perspective, darling.

5. The law of vibration –

As you know, my darling, the greatest attitude is the attitude of gratitude. In gratefulness we can all feel our wonderfulness. So for that, I have been keeping a diary since I was a cute little stardust, my dear. ⭐ I do it because it makes me connected to my very core existence.

It gives me a voice and a second eye to go through my every day life as an editor. I literally re-write my experiences by using the power of the vibration of my **gratitude** at the end of every single day, so they always stay as a "good memory" in my mental bank. Not only when I am keeping my diary, but also when I am comparing myself and my life to others, I also have my focus on my gratefulness and on the feelings that I am grateful for. It is by far, the most important comparison reference you could ever have in your life, my Shiny. Always remember this magical vibration. And it is as crucial as it is to express your gratitude to others by sharing your appreciations with them, it is just as important to express as your gratefulness for yourself, darling. How appreciative have you been to the people in your life, my Shiny dear?

6. The law of rhythm –

Rhtyhm is a dancer, dear stardust. So with the power of music, I had this rhythm in my life, darling. Wondering how? Well, I started playing flute when I was 5, mandolin when I was 6, organ when I was 8 and guitar when I was 16. 🌠 So, yes, it is true that the music had its upbeat rhythm in my life, the princess of the skies. And, yes, I used music to move in harmony with the energy of my life. But this rhythm became sacred when I opened myself into the power of the lyrics, the words, repeatedly playing in my mind as a communication tool of my body and my soul. Because, my dear Shiny, as a Pisces and an unconscious music listener, I used to love sad songs, as well!!! Oh, my! No wonder why I felt even more down when I was already feeling down! Those saddening words were just the wrong kind of input to my mind to process, darling! Sadness was becoming the vibration of my thoughts in my mind, and from my mind to my body, and from my body to my soul!!! Nooo!!! The minute I realized the power of language thanks to the number one technology of mind, NLP, I stopped that negative input to my cosmic circle, darling. And guess what??? Since I stopped listening or watching the wrong kinda rhythm, my mind starting flowing in its cosmic harmony, remembering its **universal service**, darling! I kid you not! Since I have cleaned and kept my mind away from any dark input it can receive from the outside, the physical world, I have been remembering my own cosmic, universal purpose, darling! You gotta do it!

7. The law of attraction.

I was watching 90210 in my childhood, and now I live in 90210. I saw a man in a picture wishing a man like him in my life, and I met him a few months later in another part of the world! I heard about a university with an open pool from my cousin when I was a little girl and I went to that university (METU). I wished to get an education from Harvard and I went to Harvard Business School four years later. And when I came back to LA, I wanted to have a career where I was the sole resource, talent and everything to my business, and I have been running a one-lady show since 2011. The examples can go on and on and on. So, yes, my dear, I have absolutely been **attracting very awesome things** to my Shiny galactic path with the power of my subconscious mind, darling. ⭐

8. The law of action.

I can admit that this is a special gift that I have, darling. Being a risk-taker and a brave life maker, I took one action after another after another and another in my life. Do you remember how I got my first job by just showing up at the ageny's door? Or how I got my job at The Phelps or at UCLA as an instructor, darling? I certainly had that persistence towards getting what I want in my blood somehow, dear. I literally trusted my struggle; I knew if I had proved my enthusiasm, they would appreciate it. So I kept on **taking massive action** until it made me shine, darling.⭐

And it is true that there will be times of rejection. I had many of those, too! But isn't it also true that even your mom or your dad rejected to get you what you wanted but you kept on asking or insisting or even maybe fussing about that chocolate or ice cream, darling? ⭐ So don't you see that the FEAR of rejection is nothing but an adult way of manifesting "learned helplessness," my dear Shiny? Rise above these limitations. You have greatness in you. Anytime I got rejected I thought my dear universe had a better plan for me, that everything happens for a reason, right my darling? Here is another tip for you: I knew that whatever was going to happen was going to happen. And it was not the severity of the challenges or rejections I have been faced with, but it was the speed of my recovery rate from them that made me come back to my very positive self, honey. Time to integrate all of these laws with each other.

9. The law of relativity.

Yes, I was not the only one trying to pay my rent when I chose to move to Istanbul. In fact, I was lucky that I had a place to stay and being able to have the power to pay for it! Yes, I would much rather suffer the pain of discipline to do my job to get my paycheck then losing my income in my comfortable life. And, yes, compared to so many millions in our physical world without even clean water, my challenge to look a little more fight and it was a great problem to have, my dear. Everything is relative right? Like our genious Einstein proved over half a century ago. Everything is relative. Even the color of the blue you see in the sea. And by practicing this wisdom of relativity, I reminded myself that there are other people who would give so much to be where I am or to have the problem I have. And so I remained focused on solutions rather than all these relatively big problems of mine in my path, darling. Always compare yourself with the less fortunate and keep on creating solutions for your situations.

10. The law of perpetual transmutation of energy.

My first speech as a motivational speaker was about commitment, my sparky—the commitment that I made to myself as a change agent of this planet, as well as the commitment of sodium and cloride to form the element of salt together.⭐ To be honest, this was the hardest one for me to practice since I thought I was not a person who can commit to something. I was looking at my life and seeing everything and everyone I left behind, my family, my friends, my jobs, the cities I lived, the man I married, the career I invested in.... Well, honey, again, it was just wrong thinking! ⭐ Depends on how you look at it, right? So when I look at everything now, I see an incredible galactic being chasing her cosmic dream to shine by remembering her very own universal service to others, because she is committed to her own superstar cosmic Be'ING!

***

Remember, these laws are running the whole universe, Shiny, and since you are a part of it, these laws are also running your cosmic experience every single day, honey. So it is required, expected and demanded from you that you spend your time understanding these laws by heart! Direct your focus on each and every one of them and think thoroughly about them—how they work metaphysically in our cosmos and how they can work practically in your life.

These laws, these fundamental principles of our endless shimmering universe, are the pre-requisites for you to design your conscious galactic path to shine bright with your dazzling diamond happiness, my darling. These are the cosmic secrets that are kept away from public knowledge because they are what we need to know and implement in our everyday lives if we want to achieve any kind of success and fulfillment on our planet earth. Note that there is a huge difference between success and fulfillment, my dear. Success has been figured out already; it's a science with step-by-step action plans and easy-to-implement formulae to get the results you want to get. But fulfillment—that's where you draw the line between physical beings and galactic beings, my starlight. Galactic leaders are all about leading physically, mentally, emotionally, financially, socially and spiritually fulfilled lives and sharing that wisdom with the rest of their galactic friends, while physical beings are wasting their time on earth with trying to fight their way out of darkness and are full of anger, blame and helplessness.

So again, as a galactic leader, it's your job to know the laws that govern your galaxy, honey. It's like living in Los Angeles, and not knowing what your legal rights and obligations are as a resident of California. You know the tax rate in here, right? Hope so!⭐ You know how to take the 405—like you have to stop at the red lights and at the stop signs, or before you make a right onto a new street, etc., right? Most probably.⭐ You know when it is time to file your taxes or celebrate Christmas, correct? Let me ask you, why do you know all these? Because you live in California and in order to get through your days without any problems with IRS or getting any traffic tickets from DMV you'd better know these rules and apply them carefully in every single day, right, my dear? You see, you are already applying some sun-shining California rules into your days, so why not using your God-given intelligence and stretch your focus on the big picture to understand the cosmic rules of our universe, my Shiny darling? Why not get electric into your galactic resonance, you sparky head?

We all miss these cosmic rules so easily in our every day lives, because they are not written anywhere like they are on your DMV booklets or your tax forms from IRS; you don't have red lights on the streets reminding you to stop reacting to your life, to the people or to the situations happening around you with the primitive parts of your brain. There are no departments in the banks or hospitals who are in charge of explaining how to apply the law of polarity or the law of the rhythm in our everyday physical world. So I get you. These laws were never published anywhere with the public, and that's why you never knew about them before, my galactic star. But here they are now. You know now. You know how to become a cosmically driven, globally transformed breathtaking galactic leader now! You know now that you are here to BE, so that you can DO and then you can HAVE all the tangible and intangible things you desire to HAVE in your Shiny galactic path!

And now, Shiny, it's time for me to share our 10 Galactic Rules for Galactic Leaders that I collected from the wisest galactic beings ever lived in our planet. I will explain each and every one of these galactic rules in the upcoming pages, but I am listing them here all together because they are the fundamental teachings for a galactic leader. So, you'd better take these rules very seriously and use them as practical tools to shine your path darling!

10 Galactic Rules for Galactic Leaders

1. Ask and you shall receive. (#attraction)
2. Whether you Be-Live you can, or you cannot, you are right. (#karma)
3. How you do one thing is how you do everything. (#oneness)
4. The best view is seen from above. (#perspective)
5. Where the mind goes, energy flows. (#focus)
6. **When you are in the flow, you simply glow**. (#oneness)
7. Who you surround yourself with is who you eventually become. (#proximity)
8. You may not have the resources that you need, but you will always have the resourcefulness if you seed. (#creativity)
9. Definition of insanity: Doing the same thing over and over again and expecting different results. (#creativity)
10. The queen of any of your skill is repetition my dear. (#commitment)

Your galactic life is already making more sense, right, darling? I know! Isn't it fascinating to study the meaning of your life as a galactic stardust? Well, the cosmic laws will obviously require more careful attention from you. ☆ We will revisit those laws again in the future chapters. But first we need to come back to the physical world and educate you about the principles of your mind so you can get the most out of your life as a galactic being. You know by now that your mind is your only tool to build the bridge of life between your body and your soul.

Therefore, now, please give your undivided attention and your galactic dedication to this chapter because you are about to learn the world's most powerful technology of the mind: Neuro Linguistic Programming! And you can always choose to sign up to my world class NLP certification trainings here on my website, darling: https://www.Be-LiveinU.com/.

10 Universal Principles of the Mind (NLP) For You To Let Your Power Shine Out!

1. The principle of five senses:

You observe your physical life through your five senses: Visual, Auditory, Kinesthetic, Olfactory and Gustatory senses (VAKOG). These five senses play the role of navigation in your physical worlds to find your ways in life.

In other words, every experience or memory you have in your mind has been computerized in terms of these five representational systems and stored in your temporal lobe for later on editing and re-programming purposes.

It is also very crucial to note the principle of "**4-Tuple**" that every memory that's saved in your memory bank has to have a combination of at least four of these five representational systems in it. If not, that memory is not considered a real experience. In other words, if you have not LIVED it, it is not called "experience" in your mental world. It might be information you heard from somewhere or you saw it online or you read it in a book, but it will just be information, not an experience. If only you have the 4-Tuple principle applied into that information would it be then saved as your experience.

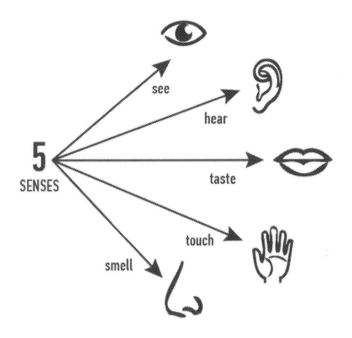

Think of a college student, studying the information that he wants to practice later in life. Can he claim that he has the experience in the field since he has been studying it for four years? Not at all! In the professional world, we understand it very well. However, when it comes to our everyday personal lives, we perfectly forget what an experience is.⭐

So, if you fall into the category of people who claim to know it all because they have been reading it, searching for and researching about it for the longest time, yet not even once fully experienced what you have been studying, it really is time to re-consider your beliefs about what "knowledge" is. Had you not tasted a watermelon ever before in your life, how could you possibly claim musk melon is more delicious than watermelon, right?

2. The principle of mind maps:

The way you store outside information from the world around you, inside of your mind with your five senses, in terms of sounds, images, feelings, smells and tastes shapes the way you organize your mental bank as your own individual mind map. And how you use these five senses— for example, storing images in colors and centering them around you or in black white and disassociated from you— makes you a unique individual, a unique, life-mapping machine. And since everyone has his own unique way of mapping his own five senses and organizing them in his own unique way with his already existing beliefs, values, goals and cosmic characters he is with, everyone becomes so unique and so distinct. And that results in each and every being of this universe to be a unique being, naturally very different from one other in the way that he observes life and create his own individual reality according to his own observation of the reality.

So there is no "one reality" that is the same and valid for all the beings of this planet. There is no "one single truth of life" that you need to live by, or learn from others, including mine. You have the power to choose to whatever you want to Be-Live in. My truth of life that I am sharing with you is that you are a piece of galactic stardust just as part of the big, cosmic universe, and if you can study and understand how the universe works in her cosmic intelligence, then you can absolutely Be-Live in U and let your cosmic power shine out!

So, there is only your own reality and your own truth for you to Be-Live in and create to live in, darling. Of course, there are some universal rules like the law of gravity, (the law of attraction), polarity, relativity, cause and effect, etc. However, apart from these very valid universal laws, you are meant to obtain your own laws of your galactic life. And for that purpose, the way you use your mind map to observe and filter your life is one of your biggest powers as a galactic leader to shine! And in order to have the most powerful mind map, you must have the most powerful beliefs and values that are in line and supportive of your galactic goals.

Well, the rest of our galactic principles for your mind are some of the most powerful beliefs for you to **Be-Live in U** and shine like a galactic superstar, my dear:

3. The principle of the power of focus:

Your mind map that you develop during the time of your life enables you to look at life in a certain perspective. And if your mind is flexible enough, you have the ability to shift your perspective about life, to create the best cosmic approach as humanly possible. Basically, the flexibility of your mind is the power of your focus. And the power of your focus is totally a conscious choice of your galactic mind. So much so that, just with the power of your focus— no matter what happens in life—you have the ability to change the way you look at it with the power of your focus. And this ability of changing the way you look at life is much more valuable than what happens to you in your life.

To put it in numbers, whatever happens to you in life represents only 10 percent of your reality, and your ability to change the way you look at what happens represents the remaining 90 percent of your reality. Just like the cosmic law of correspondence, the 10 percent is what you see as your physical reality. However there is this huge 90 percent of the spiritual reality that you don't get to see. So that's why you must have the ability to shift your focus in your galactic path, in order to get in touch and get connected to the 90 percent of spirituality.

4. The principle of the power of knowledge:

Knowledge, thought, memory and imagination are all the results of sequences and combinations and permutations of the way you filter and store information. If you learn what those sequences, combinations and permutations are, then you will have the ability to influence what's working for you and what's not, eventually creating better solutions for your goals in life.

Let's look at the sequence of knowledge for example.

There are <u>four levels of learning in a healthy human mind</u>:

1) <u>Unconscious Incompetent (UI):</u> The level that you don't even know what you don't know.
2) <u>Conscious Incompetent (CI):</u> The level that you become aware of what you don't know.
3) <u>Conscious Competent (CC):</u> The level that you get good at what you used to not know.
4) <u>Unconscious Competent UC):</u> Having a skill and you don't even know about it.

In the first level, **Unconscious Incompetence**, since we all operate from a place of knowledge-less-ness, we consistently and dangerously judge things. Remember the 4-tuple principle of an experience? Your knowledge needs to be measured through four of your five senses for a real recorded experience in your mind, right? If not, then you are simply judging, or, in other words, you are assuming. ☆ You are assuming why your boss is acting toward you the way he does. You are assuming why your mom tells you what she tells you. You are assuming how your friends feel about you. But the worst is, you are assuming that the world you live in is a world of your thoughts, your values, your beliefs, your goals, your strengths and your insecurities. Of course you will do that, honey! That's what you assume with what you have inside of your head! You don't know what others have in their heads. You don't know how it feels to live in someone else's head with someone else's life experiences, values, beliefs and goals. And you don't really know what you don't know about them, about being and living like them. That's why they are already taken and you have "you" to be and live in, darling.

By the way, can you imagine every single person on earth having her own judgments and her own assumptions of what life is about and how it should be for you, too? And can you also imagine every single person trying to impose what she believes (assume) on each other, including you? Are you one of those, honey? Trying to tell others what to do, what to say, how to sit or how to stand in life, even though nobody is asking for your opinion? If you have been, you are now aware that what you know has its meaning for you and only you because you are coming from your own point of view; so keeping your mouth shut can definitely be a better practice in understanding and respecting other people's life styles, especially when they are not asking for your opinion. If they are asking for your opinion and you are telling them what to do and how to do it because they are asking, it's a little better place to be. But still, if you don't know how to ask the right questions to understand her position in life, and if you are not trained in mind-mapping and coaching, it's a great possibility that you might not help them or, even worse, mislead them.

I find this very fascinating. Let me ask you: Have you ever tried to operate a surgery on someone if you are not a doctor? Have you ever claimed that you can write the best software programs if you are not a computer programmer? Or have you ever tried to teach someone how to ski if you haven't even done it yourself? I hope you all answered "no" to these questions. ☆ Simply because these are obvious fields that we need the expert's opinion and we cannot do it ourselves, right? These are obvious **Conscious Incompetence** areas that we know what we don't know about. On the other hand, when it comes to the areas like life in general, communications, relationships, emotional management, personal growth and change-work, we simply Be-Live (assume) that we are at the level of **Conscious Competence**, even though we are at the very UI level of not even having a clue of what we don't know about ourselves, about others, about our motivations, about why we do what we do, about how the mind works and about how we can become a better version of ourselves, etc. Isn't that crazy?

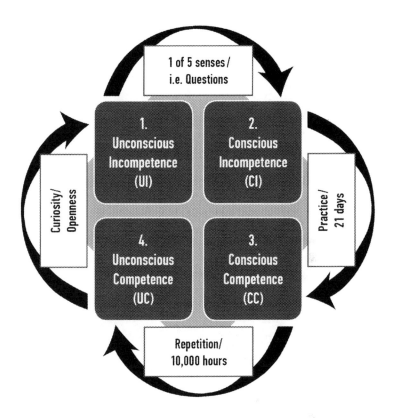

These four levels of learning can be seen by looking at any skill that you have. For example, let's talk about learning about the five components of emotional intelligence. Your first step into learning anything new is to become aware that you don't know anything about it and you want to learn about it. How do you become aware about something you don't know? Well, a simple question from a friend, a teacher or an article you read somewhere would work. 🌟 With that simple question, you already pass on to the second step. This second level is CI, knowing that you didn't know the five components of emotional intelligence before. But wait a minute. What is Emotional Intelligence? Right? So you realize that you heard something about it but you don't really know what it means. And you want to know about it. So you basically invite the neurons of your galactic mind to work and do a little search for you. You first ask Google or go get a book about it and start reading. The more you read the more you are hooked. Next thing you know, this is your new passion. You want to talk about your new passion, you start conversations about it, you ask people questions about it, you explain what it is to them, and so on and so forth. And this level right here is the level in which you are competent and knowledgeable. However, you still know it with your conscious level, which means that the knowledge you have about the Emotional Intelligence is something like your knowing how to bake a cake. You know what's needed as ingredient, but you don't really know what the degree of the oven you need is to bake your cake or how many minutes it needs to bake. So you can't really tell who around you has the highest Emotional Intelligence yet because you need more practice. And in time, with practice—with 10,000 hours of practice, to be more precise—you can finally reach the level of mastery. This is the unconsciousness competence level, where you do it by heart with your unconscious mind because you don't really your need your conscious thinking mind any more. Your body learns it and does it automatically for you, and that's what we call, my dear, a level of "mastery."

So just like this example, the principle of knowledge can be summarized with this analogy: **if you don't have it, then you cannot give it**. If you don't have the information and the knowledge available in your mind for growth and excellence, you can't grow or excel at anything.

You must have the desire, the curiosity, the openness and the willingness to learn and expand the horizons of your knowledge to grow and excel at anything in life so you can enlarge your level of being from Unconscious Incompetence to Unconscious Competence.

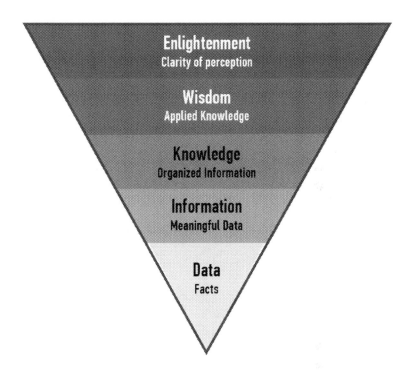

5. The principle of worthiness:

Human beings have all the tools and resources within to affect a change in their lives. Well, it is, of course, related with the universal law of oneness and it has some ties with the law of action. Since you are a galactic leader made of stardust, you are meant to shine. All you have to do is again to Be-Live in U and let your power shine out!

Most of the time, this is not how the story ends. Because all of humanity's biggest fear is the fear of not being good enough. FEAR by the way, stands for FALSE EVIDENCE

APPEARING REAL. ☆ So every time you feel close to fear of "not being good enough," remember the acronym and that'll do it I Be-Live!☆

Yes, you are good enough and you are worthy of love, respect, success, abundance, growth and excellence in your galactic path. You know why? Well, the creator made you perfect, that's why. God makes no mistakes and you are one of God's miracles. If you need more proof, just remember that you have about 60,000 miles long of vessels in your human body, which is enough to go 2.5 times around the world! And you have this perfect system of re-creation that is happening as you are reading these lines right now. Millions of your cells are dying and billions of new ones are being created. Plus, you don't even need to think about breathing in. Your heart does it on its own, by default. Isn't that awesome? Or would you prefer having the full control of your breathing instead? Even if you did, you might end up dying since you are too busy focusing on unimportant things. So I am not really sure if you could handle such fatal responsibility on top of all those worries in your head. What do you think? Would you like to be totally responsible about ordering the right amount of hormones to your brain for your lungs and your kidneys every millisecond of your existence? Or do you prefer your cosmic system handle it for you? ☆I guess we have a common understanding now.

You do have all that it takes to make every impossible possible, because you are impossible to start with! Look at your own system inside, for God's sake!

6. The principle of communication:

The meaning of your communication is measured by the feedback you receive. This principle is about your ability to influence yourself and others through the way you communicate with yourself and others. If you can have this belief very close to your heart, you can really create miracles with it.

It's true that we may not be able to create the same level of influence as we want all the time, but, with the help of this belief, you will be keeping track of the effect of your communication and measuring the metrics around it.

So here are the three components of communication as a study and metric area for you to consider when you are working on improving the quality of your communication:

1. Content: This is what you really say.
2. Tone of voice: This is the verbal quality of HOW you say it.
3. Body language: This is the non-verbal qualities of HOW you say it.

Communication

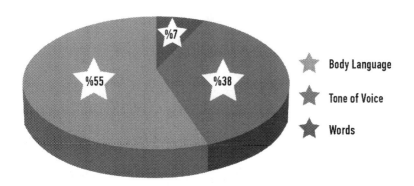

As you see, your communication is not really about what you say, it's more about HOW you say it to the person you are communicating with, including yourself, to get the best results out of it. Just remember, you can only measure the influence of your communication by looking at the feedbacks and results that you receive with it. So if there is anything you can do to improve any of these three areas, go ahead and measure the results and do something about it.

7. The principle of needs:

There are always positive intentions behind all kinds of actions in the world. What a belief to embrace, right? Well, this principle is about understanding the psychology of human behaviors and the reasons and motivations behind them. It may sound weird when you first read it and try to understand it, but it will make more sense, especially when the chapter of "BEING" is read. In that chapter, which is your second step in to Be-Live in U, I will talk about the Fulfillment Theory of a Galactic Leader in detail, and everything will become clearer by then.

What you can do by now is that you can think about the idea of having this new belief that behind every action there is positive intention. And the reason for the intention being positive is because the intention is about the fulfillment of a physiological, emotional or psychological need by the person who is taking the action.

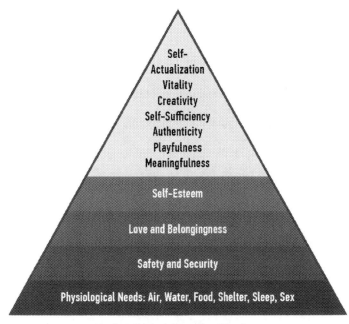

Self-
Actualization
Vitality
Creativity
Self-Sufficiency
Authenticity
Playfulness
Meaningfulness

Self-Esteem

Love and Belongingness

Safety and Security

Physiological Needs: Air, Water, Food, Shelter, Sleep, Sex

Abraham Maslow- Hierarchy of Needs

8. The principle of behavior:

This principle of Neuro Linguistic Programming is a fundamental belief about human behaviors. It states that every human being is worthy and valuable for her existence as a human being. However, her behaviors may not be that worthy, appropriate or valuable when measured against the results that they get in their own lives and in others' lives from those behaviors. So it's necessary that you measure your behaviors according to the results you get from them and according to the results you intended to get in the first place.

And it's also very important to note that, when measuring behaviors, you spend only 20 percent of your time in analyzing the reasons of the problem, challenge or the idea and the remaining 80 percent in creating alternative solutions for your challenge and idea.

How do you measure behaviors? Well, here is a great chart for your practical use:

CLASS OF BEHAVIOR	YOU ENJOY DOING IT	GOOD FOR YOU	GOOD FOR OTHERS	GOOD FOR HUMANITY
A CLASS	★	★	★	★
B CLASS		★	★	★
C CLASS			★	★
D CLASS	★		★	★
E CLASS	★	★		★
F CLASS				

So go ahead and measure your current behaviors. Anything less than B is not really where you want to be, right? Well how about the behaviors of others around you? I hope you don't have Ds. We will re-visit the qualification of human behaviors in the future chapters because it is very important to know what we are doing and what really we are causing, don't you think?

At least now you know how to measure and manage your behaviors, so you can use this chart as a belief, as a technique (you don't really use any techniques unless you Be-Live in them anyways), next time when you are deciding on a new behavior in your life.

9. The principle of 6W+1H:

This principle relates with the time's popular concept of "**Contextual Intelligence**" by Harvard Business Review: https://hbr.org/2014/09/contextual-intelligence. And NLP is the best model to apply the Contextual Intelligence, because it questions the contextual framework behind human communications and behaviors and formulizes that framework into small chunks of information. The chunking technique that is used for this purpose is extremely simple yet undeniably powerful:

In any given information, you must be able to answer these contextual questions, or the information is not whole and prone to high degree of subjectivity, miscommunication and misunderstanding:

WHAT:
WHY:
WHEN:
WHERE:
WHO:
WHAT IS THE SOURCE/WHERE IS THE RESOURCE:
HOW:

So when communicating with someone, it's your responsibility to be clear about all these aspects of the information you are giving and receiving. Because not everybody is aware about this principle; they don't even know that they don't know this. So that's why it's your responsibility to make sure the communication is clear, specific and precise both ways honey.

Haven't you ever seen an old friend somewhere and you both went: "We should meet up! Oh, yes, definitely" and another five years pass and you never meet? ☆ It's simply a lack of **WHEN** in your communication my darling. It is simply failing to plan it. By the way, where else is this same pattern showing up in your life? Not scheduling your goals?

You know, Shiny, galactic leaders are schedulers. If there is anything they want to do, they simply take their smart phones and schedule it to their agenda, right there and then! It is such an incredible cosmic power to have, my darling! Way to go!

Or how about the MISSING RESOURCE in conversations? I love this one; it's pretty entertaining. ☆ You know sometimes people talk about a new diet that they heard from somewhere or from someone that is supposed to make you lose all your weight and make you look younger at the same time? But they never think about WHAT IS THE SOURCE of this diet? Is this a clinical study after 15 years? Which university or institution is involved in this diet, etc.? And they simply buy into the idea because of its promises and never make their own research about the promises, if it is good for their conditions, or if it suits their purposes, their life styles, etc.

Another common problem in communication is the lack of WHO in our conversations. Say you are talking to a very good friend of yours that you trust and have fun together. And you are asking her opinion about a big change you want to do in your life. And she is a person of certainty: ☆She has worked at the same job for over 12 years, she has been married to the same guy for 17 years, and she goes to the same places and does the same things every weekend. ☆of course, she tells you why you shouldn't change anything and be happy with what you have. ☆What do you think is happening here, darling? Not surprising, right?

So be selective in asking people's opinions according to WHO they are and how they lead their lives, my sparky head. She can be a great person to learn how to sustain work life, marriage, etc., but, as you see from this example, she may not be and is definitely not the best person to consult in creating big life changes. You go ask people who have changed their lives and enjoy it, people who know how to do it.

YOU ARE A STAR!
BE SELECTIVE

Similar to the diagram of the principle of information, we do have another diagram called "The Johari Window" to demonstrate the principle of 6W+1H knowledge in its clarity to us and to others. Let's talk about this chart a little bit:

THE JOHARI WINDOW

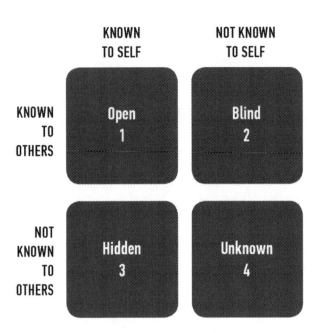

In the first place of "OPEN," you have the information about you that's clear to you and clear to others. You know who you are and why you do what you do and so do the people around you. For example you Be-Live that you are a happy person and you lead a happy life and people around you can witness it, see it and so can measure it, especially from your Facebook. ⭐

In the second window of "BLIND," you have some communication and behaviors that you are not aware of, but others are. An example would be your getting nervous and losing your confidence under stress at work. To you, it is just a lot of things to do and that's the way you handle them. But for others, the way you handle them might mean their broken hearts, hurt feelings and disliking your personality. And unless you ask them how they feel or they give you feedback about their perception of your behaviors, you are blind to all that.

In the third window of "HIDDEN," you intentionally hide how you feel, what you do or how you do it from others and, therefore, they are unaware of your hidden agenda. For example, people may Be-Live that you have a comfortable life since you show up to fancy restaurants, shop from fancy stores and are generous to your friends. But you do it because you owe thousands $$$ to your credit cards, not because you are leading a financial comfort in your life.

And in the final quadrant of The Johari Window is called the "UNKNOWN" window. This is the area neither you nor people around you are aware of. If you are wondering how it could be possible, think about something you have never done—singing, for example. You are unaware if you have a great talent in singing because you have never tried it before. And since you have never done it and it's not known to you, it is also not known to others because there is no way for them to measure this for you.

Got it, my Shiny? Maybe it is time for you to try different things so you can discover your next million-dollar talent in you! ⭐

YOU ARE A STAR!
TRY SOMETHING NEW

10. The principle of feedback:

As we already discussed, the effect of your communication is the feedback you receive from others or the results you get in your life. So the principle of feedback suggests the same formulation for your behaviors: There is no failure, there is only feedback. And there are results from your prior actions that you can measure to learn and grow from.

I know it may not be so easy for you to look at your bankruptcy as a feedback or something to learn from, but that really is what it is. If you really Be-Live in it. You must be able to use the power of your focus right here and shift your perspective from, *"What happened and why did it happen this way?"* to, *"Whatever has happened just happened. No meanings or emotions are attached. What can I learn from what happened so that I never do it again? Or, better yet, how can I create a growth opportunity from all this?"* Because, there are results, so there must be measurements and learnings from all that. This kind of thinking, a definitely "from above," unattached to the losses and a totally galactic kind of way must be the way you look at your happenings in life—any happenings. Because, remember, the best view is seen from the top.🌟

There is a reason why galaxies are up in the sky, so there must also be a reason why galactic leaders are at the top, darling, don't you think? So isn't it true that as you rise up you get a wider perspective? Don't you like what you see better when you are taking a helicopter tour up in the clouds vs. what you see when you are looking at the helicopters down from the ground (*assuming that you have taken a helicopter tour*)? Again there is a reason for it, the enlargement of the perspective, the view from the top, the vision of a galactic leader!

Now, you can begin to relax, my dear Shiny, because I am going to make this superstar process of *letting your galactic power shine out* really easy for you!  With my step-by-step Shiny and happy galactic guidance, clarifying and awareness-building exercises and your own dedicated desire to shine bright like an electric sky diamond, you will be able to learn how to apply some really fascinating galactic leader tools and techniques into your life. And you will immediately start to shine and dazzle the world out very dramatically, my dear!

So are you ready? Let's go then!

YOU ARE A STAR!
GET READY

Now, to start with, I want you to think about how you draw a star. You know, how you connect those five edgy, curvy lines together on a paper and they make a STAR. And now imagine how a star shines! It goes bling bling, right? So shimmery and so glittering. Well, that's what a galactic leader does, darling, it shines!!! Or maybe I should have said, SHE SHINES! And that's what exactly we are going to do with you! We are gonna make you shine!

For you to shine bright like an incredible galactic diamond, my dear Shiny, there are five galactic vacations you need to take both your heart and your mind to. Each vacation you will heartfully take is going to enlighten a starry part of yours, freeing you from shadiness and shakiness caused by the uncertain feelings about your path that you might have been holding onto. And each step you will mentally take is going to make your Shiny head ready to think like a superstar so that you can start shining on, my dear darling! So, now get excited, my fireball! You are about to explode! ⭐

These are the five galactic steps you will be taking to unleash the galactic leader in you and to let your stardust power immediately shine out:

WE ARE HERE TO FEEL ALIVE.

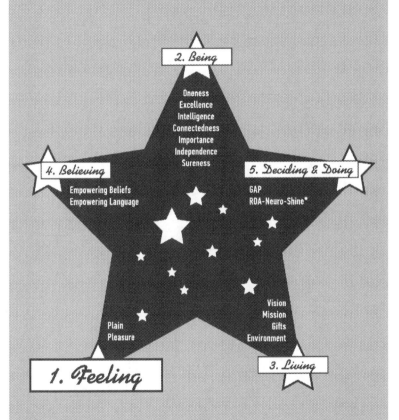

1. FEELING

You know that your time has come to shine! You really feel it deep inside. You hear the calling, your true calling from the universe. And so you FEEL that something's gotta change! But do you know what you really want to change, Shiny? Do you know what exactly you want in life? Because most others don't, darling. Sadly, they have no idea what their little juicy heart beats for. And I would really encourage you to think deeply about your passion, my dear. Think really deeply and clearly. Think about how you used to respond to those aunts and uncles wondering about what you would do when you grow up, when you were a tiny, little stardust in your own shimmery galactic world! ⭐

Go back to those stardust years of yours for one second. Remember what you used to enjoy doing, watching, reading, listening, etc., when you really had the choice as a little kid. Anything that made you FEEL really HAPPY! And the reason I am saying, *"When you really had a choice"* is because when we were kids, we were really good at knowing what we wanted and what we didn't want, and we simply FELT free to choose whatever it was that we wanted. Remember those times as a little kiddo? We were only concerned about how to FEEL better and how to have more fun at any given time and place! Go back to those times in your Shiny little head and I know you will remember. You knew exactly what you wanted, and where, when, how and even with whom you wanted it. Well, I am not really sure about the WHY though. 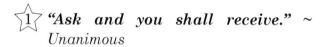 You may not have known the reason behind your wants and desires, but who cared then, right? You just knew what you wanted and that was it! Because knowing what you wanted and asking/insisting/fussing/ obsessing about it pretty much solved a big deal of your problems in your life as a cute little stardust. Didn't it my dear? As a result, I Be-Live you understand all that *"ask and you shall receive"* universal formulation by now my dear, correct? This is our first galactic rule to follow:

☆1☆ *"Ask and you shall receive."* ~ *Unanimous*

How easy that was as a kiddo, wasn't it? Because today, most of the human creatures seem to have forgotten to apply this simple formulation to their adult lives, since they are being awarded and rewarded for knowing what they want and going after it. Isn't that an irony, my darling?

Well, I find it a very galactic leader attitude! ☆ When you FEEL that your time has come to shine, knowing what you don't want will help you to a great extent. However, knowing exactly what you want will magically set you FREE, my dear Queen B! Free of all the unwanted emotions, all the unpleasant situations, and all the darkness that you are trying to weed through in order to find your clarity and let your purpose to shine through! Sounds fantastic, doesn't it? ☆

YOU ARE A STAR!

ASK AND YOU
SHALL RECEIVE

And so, my question is, do you wanna fly away from an existing PAIN or wanna shine towards a spectacular PLEASURE to find your purpose, my dear? How do you FEEL, right here, right now as you are stepping into your galactic path?

Because in the end, here are the **two galactic feelings** that any decision of a Shiny galactic leader comes down to:

> **Pain**

> Pain, pain, pain. The global nightmare for all of humanity; the devastating stopper of every big dream; the reason behind all the fights, resentments, jealousies, procrastinations, failures, inactions and re-actions; the irresistible urge to be right, the undeniable force to live tight; the death of all the great ideas; and many, many more things. What are you gonna do, honey? That's just the way we are! And that's why they call it the name of the game! No pain no gain.

> Well, in life, people need either inspiration or desperation. Sadly and obviously, desperation works millions of times better than inspiration does for making people move, for getting them to make decisions and to act upon them! Oh yes, Shiny, pain

has the biggest power to move your sexy wings! Pain is the strongest WHY in a lot of people's lives. Pain overcomes the hardest challenges that pleasure can literally not. And thus, pain is the most miraculous TEACHER for all the beings of this wonderful universe.

Because, we as all the galactic beings, including human beings, are hard-wired to survive and to be alive. So keeping away from any potential danger and running away from any kind of unpleasant, fear-related feelings will always serve your primary purpose of existence. Always, my dear!

FEAR, my Shiny, stands for False Evidence Appearing Real. Remember that, Sweetie? And here are the top two *False Evidences Appearing Real* in the planet earth:

1. **Not being good enough**
2. **Not being loved enough**

Oh, so dramatic. Can you relate to these unpleasant feelings, my galactic friend? You know sometimes you feel alone among all the other bling bling sky-mates of yours. You feel like you are the only one galactic creature left outside of your Shiny path, with your own unpleasant feelings towards your existence. Or for some incredible reasons you feel less than who you really are sometimes, as if you are never good enough to belong to the world of infinite possibilities up in the sky. Or as if you are never Shiny enough to give birth to your magical superstar identity inside of you. Copy that?

So just don't copy these feelings, my darling. Because these are false feelings! They are not real. Those are

FEAR-FULL feelings. If they were real, you would see them, you would hear them or you may be able to touch them. But they are not. They are all in your Shiny head, my darling! Wake up!!! And realize that everything you are running away from, is in your head, my dearest little Shiny. It is nonsense obviously. You can't run away from yourself, can you? So stop running away from your very natural not-so-pleasant feelings and start loving them. ☆
I know it sounds crazy to ask a galactic leader to embrace and love her fears—or false feeling evidences, better said—but just do it! Because you can! You know what an earthy guru said once:

☆2 *"Whether you think you can or you cannot, you are right."* ~ Henry Ford

So, just think that you can and you will, my sparkly, you certainly will. If you need evidence, just think about all the things that you thought you could never do. All the things that you wanted to be, to do and to have. But just because you had that poor belief of yours, somewhere up in your dark spaces, that you could never ever be, do or have those things, you haven't even tried doing anything about them, have you, my darling? Which means you haven't even triggered your nervous system to come to work and support you with that belief, right? Instead, you have unconsciously ordered all of your neurons with your magical intelligence, to stay just as stagnant as they are and do nothing crazy, so that you could prove to yourself that you are not good enough to do those things or have those things! Because remember, whether you Be-Live you can or you cannot, you are right! Get it, my Shiny? Do you now see the vicious circle running in your sparkly head?

Well, I don't have any other questions, your honor. This case is permanently dropped!

And now, think about all the other things that you thought you could actually do, even though others told you that you couldn't, but still you did! Why? Because you simply chose to Be-Live that you could do it, instead of that you couldn't do it, Isn't that right, my sparkly head? Isn't that too simple as a galactic rule? ⭐ And guess what. Just because others challenged you with your belief, perhaps you did more than you normally would with the urge to prove yourself right, unconsciously ordering each and every cell of you to war against the outside resistance towards your own belief inside. Sound familiar?

Yes, we do that, fireball. Neurologically speaking, when you feel threatened by anyone, any situation or anything that challenges your beliefs in your Shiny head, every inch of you gets fired up to fight against that threat. And by winning that war, you proudly prove yourself that your fear of *"not being good enough"* is false evidence. And you are good enough, you are worthy and you do have the power to Be-Live that you can do anything you want to do! That's the way it goes, my Shiny ...

How about that crunchy, achy feeling of *"not being loved enough,"* my cute little thing? Aa Ooo! I almost see the sad face you are trying to imitate as you hear my words, sweetie. It's OK if you felt like this before. I have got news for you, my sparkly. You are not alone! There are millions of other galactic beings like you reading this book right now and they are all nodding their heads! We have all felt like this before! We all mistakenly thought that people getting angry at us at home or at work, or other human beings that made us feel special disappearing on us and leaving us alone meant that we are not worthy of their love. We all, at some point, suffered from love dis-ease in our lives. Perhaps by bursting into tears or crying out extremely loud like a Japanese earthquake, that's even OK. ⭐ You know why? Because we didn't know any better! We thought that we should have done some certain things or acted in some certain ways so that we would be loved. Maybe when we were little as stardust, our parents told us to behave in a certain way so that they would buy us candies or toys, and BOOM, we distorted the whole "behaving" input in such a way as to cripple ourselves later in life with this dis-ease! I hope not! But it happens, and it might have happened to your little sparky head as well, my dear.

So, now that you are aware that the FEAR of *"not being loved enough"* is also false evidence appearing real, you can easily begin to make peace with these feelings and start loving them. ⭐ Why do you need to love them? Well, haven't you heard of that idiom recommending you to keep your friends close and keep your enemies even closer, my dear? If these unpleasant feelings of yours that we call FEAR were your enemies, you would wanna get to know them, be aware of them and so that you could take control of them, right, my Shiny? Just like one of our galactic rules says:

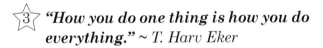

⭐ **"How you do one thing is how you do everything."** ~ *T. Harv Eker*

So the same rule applies here, sweetie: You gotta keep your positive feelings close, all around, all the time, but keep your deepest FEARS even closer, my dear. So that you can analyze them and measure them. You gotta get to know how they are appearing and disappearing, increasing or decreasing, etc., so you can develop techniques to manage them effectively and to your own benefit. After all, you cannot manage anything that you cannot measure, my dear smarty pants! ⭐ So take over your control and take it over with love dear ⭐

YOU ARE A STAR!
SMILE THROUGH
THE PAIN

Plus, when you start loving your fears, your fears will magically start loving you back! And eventually there won't be any more FEARS! There will be only LOVE between you and your PAIN related unpleasant feelings, leading you to get in touch with them, communicate with them and learn from them! What a utopic state to be! Can you imagine loving your FEAR of rejection, my dear Shiny? ⭐ Hihi! ⭐ Can you love your weaknesses? Can you still love the part of you that screwed up in that gigantic sales meeting messed up your speech in an international conference? Can you love yourself unconditionally? Hope so! ⭐

So LOVE your FEARS, my Shiny. They are also YOU! Love them! Understand what they are trying to tell you and learn from them! They exist for a reason; they have a message to share with you. Listen to them! Give them a big hug and smile at them! ⭐ If you don't love them, they will even grow bigger in you, taking control over some precious parts of you in the heart and the mind. Because they are also living organisms with chemical neural interactions among each other, they will grow stronger each and every day without your awareness, dulling your sparkle and creating shades and darkness in your Shiny little head, my darling.

So love them. When you love your fears, you will love yourself more, my Shiny. LOVE is the enchanting power to sweep all the pain away to infinity and it is the only way for you to let your inner power shine out! ⭐

> ➤ **Pleasure**

> Oh, pleasure, pleasure! Oh, darling! Aren't we all longing for it? Aren't we all living for it? With every bite we take from that delicious strawberry cheesecake, with every color-matching shoe and bag combination that we can ever create, and with every romantic and deeply hypnotic French connection we initiate⭐, don't we all go for that irresistible feeling of pleasure? Yes, we do, darling. And, yes, we will always do, my darling.⭐

Because we, the galactic beings, are nothing but spiritual machines that run with physiological and emotional needs along with our spiritual feelings. Pleasure happens to be the departmental name of all the Shiny happy feelings like LOVE, JOY and HAPPINESS that constantly feed our being. Because pleasure is the galactic label for being here in this moment and knowing that we exist with the feeling called *"being alive."*

Oo la la, Shiny, let's cheer for all the pleasure, all the love and the joy and the happiness that we have in our lives, shall we, my dear? Hence, everything we do, to have more pleasure in our lives requires a great amount of self-awareness, confidence and courage to bear all the challenges we might face along the way of getting it. Being in this state of mind is the most powerful and the most desirable of all!

YOU ARE A STAR!
FEEL PLEASURE

If you are where you are today, consider yourself lucky and move on to your path to shine, my little stardust. Because with that level of self-belief and faith in the cosmic power, you are already unstoppable!

But if some reason you feel unsure about where you are today or where you are going tomorrow, then get ready, my Shiny. We have some work to do together! And as I said before, you can keep calm and move on with a superstar attitude because I am going to make this really easy for you! ⭐

We are going to start with analyzing where you are today and how you feel about yourself, your life as a whole, other beings around you, the level of your positive feelings, etc. And for that, you will only answer some questions that I, as your Queen B, have prepared for you. ⭐

So now, my dear Shiny, please grab a pen that you really like and feel emotionally attached to, and start answering the following questions as the first step into shining your path along. And, please, you are not fooling anyone here; you are all by yourself in your own galactic energy house. So be horizontally and vertically open and honest with your shining self, darling. OK?

By the way, in case you were wondering, you will be activating new galactic cells and creating new neuro-pathways in your Shiny mind by answering these questions. Isn't that spectacular, my dear? I know that you are all about getting to know more about your Shiny wings and polishing them even more with power and glamour. So, let's begin shaping your shining success path, darling; a SUPERSTAR needs to be born out of your Shiny little edges!

Are you ready? OK, take the deepest breath ever, and let's go!

*(Time for **Rihanna's "Shine Bright Like A Diamond"** song)*

1. Life is_____
2. People are_____
3. I am_____
4. I mostly feel like_____
    in my everyday life.
5. I am **passionate about**_____
6. I love **doing**_____
    and I get to do that every day in my life!
7. I love **being**_____
    and I get to be like that every day in my life!

8. I want to do_____
   but I can't do it now because I don't have the **time**
   for it.
9. I want to do_____
   but I can't do it now because I don't have the **money**
   for it.
10. I want to do_____
    but I can't do it nowbecause I **don't know how** to
    do it.
11. I hate doing_____
    but I still <u>have to do</u> it in my everyday life.
12. If I had a chance, I would absolutely change_____
    in my life.

So how did it go? If you are ready to analyze your life
at a glance, my darling, this is how you will do it:

The first three questions are the biggest filters in your
Shiny little head, shaping the way you see yourself, your
own galaxy that you live in, your own experience that
you keep feeling, and the other beings around you, and
affecting the way you are experiencing yourself and your
galactic life. Well, if all of your answers are positive, then
great news! You are literally glittering! So keep calm and
shine on, darling! ⭐

YOU ARE A STAR!
SHINE ON

And if your answers to the first three questions above are not very positive, still keep calm, darling. We have magical ways to polish your sparkly little head along with the language that comes out of it, that we call **Neuro Linguistic Programming**, a.k.a. **NLP!**

Your answer to question #4 obviously reflects how you really feel about yourself in your galactic experience. Gotta watch out, though. We sometimes tend to forget the beauty of a smile we put on another being because we don't look at it when we are asked to measure our everyday feelings. And just because we momentarily forget it or we look at other things instead of these beauties, we tend to see the other things that we are looking at, instead of the beauties right here, right now, all promising.

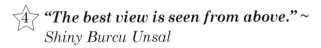 *"The best view is seen from above."* ~ *Shiny Burcu Unsal*

Which means that you gotta rise up every now and then to get a better view and to get a wider perspective about anything in life. Isn't that unbelievably elevating, my dear? Remember your beautiful wings. You have wings, dusty! You have five edgy, glossy and magnificent wings to take you higher and higher in life. And the secret is using those wings! Just like what we discussed about the life-changing difference between decisions and actions, there is also a planet-size difference between knowledge and practice. Ironically, in our galaxy, we do have a common sense about almost everything. But sadly, we barely have any practice in what we know as common sense, my darling. It's just ironic, sad and funny to be in such a situation. Who wants that? Keep calm, rise up, see the view from above and adopt a new common practice, right?⭐ Awesome!⭐

YOU ARE A STAR!
RISE UP

We are at question number 5! And your answer has the value of a million galactic diamonds, my dear Shiny. This is your WHY to fly so high, darling. If you have clarity at number 5, your electric power inside will always be on—for you to shine on! ⭐On the other hand, if you are unsure about what you are passionate about, then sit tight, Be-Live that you are only Shiny happy book away from finding it, and keep on reading, darling.

Oh, of course, it would be a tremendous help to make a list all of the things you would do for free! The things that you find easy, joyful and fun! Perhaps you always dreamed about becoming a singer, but even the idea itself was too big for you to reach that you didn't even share it with anybody. You didn't even put that idea into words to express it! Why? Well, there might be several reasons and several other "excuses." It might be that you didn't really

Be-Live in yourself that you were good enough to dare to sing in front of all those hundreds of human beings. Or, perhaps, your parents were way too conservative to let you become a singer and they held you back. Only you would know the real reason, right, Shiny? If you really deeply, passionately wanted something and you didn't follow your glowing light, only you would know it.

Be brutally honest with yourself, sweetheart. No hiding behind candy bars this time, OK? Your galactic years are counted and given to you. Remember that. So you have only one shot to make it glamorous, honey! And this is it!

Well, well, well. Here we are at questions number 6 and 7! These two are your ecstasies, my dear. Can you feel it? Aren't we talking about feelings as your first step to shine? So feel free to feel your ecstasy, Shiny! This is where you want to be! The meaning of your galactic life is to be at number 6 and 7, consistently. If you are already here consistently, you might as well stop reading my secret formula to empower your wings to fly and start writing your own formula for bliss and shine in life! Although, a truly consistent bliss and happiness is almost against your Shiny and glossy nature. ☆It is just the way you are created, my darling.☆ But it doesn't mean that you can be there nine times out of 10! You can! That works!  I Be-Live it's achievable and realistic to aim for it.

If you are not there yet, then I'll ask you to measure where you are in relation to that kind of bliss, out of 10 (1 being the lowest); anything above 6 is acceptable. For the numbers below 6, you must really find out what's not working in your life. You must be feeling a lot of pressure, a lot of burdens and maybe even "stuck" if you are below 6. Well, that's not the FEELING you need to be feeling in your Shiny path, darling, not at all! And you know that!

Therefore, you must be focusing immediately on measuring the quality of your life with the stardom of life exercise in the following pages! By doing that exercise, you will be able to specify what exactly is lowering your score and what you really have to change in your life so that you won't have to tolerate being here, right honey?

Galactic leaders don't tolerate anything less than excellence, my dear. Just saying.

YOU ARE A STAR!

EXAMINE WHAT YOU TOLERATE

Oh, and, please tell me that you have not written anything for the rest of the questions number 8, 9, 10, 11 and 12! Because if you did, you have literally declared that it sucks to be you! ☹Are you really OK with experiencing a life that is making you list all those excuses for the things that really matter to you, for the things you hate doing and but are still imprisoning yourself with them and feeling like you don't have any other choice? Really? And then you go ahead and call what you experience as "life"? Hmmm.... Think again, sweetheart. If that's life, then what others are living with no answers to these five questions and very awesome and powerful answers to the first seven questions?

No, no, no, Shiny! This is a danger zone, honey. Don't you hear the sirens already? Oh, my! You don't wanna be here, living your life less than your beautiful soul deserves, darling! You know what you really deserve and how much more happiness, fulfillments and light you wanna feel in your galactic path! Because you are born to live with passion darling, not with tension!

So please take action and, better yet, take tons of actions, NOW! Immediately!

YOU ARE A STAR!
TAKE ACTION

Well, speaking about taking action, as you know by now, you will only take action when you really make a decision, which I will take you through as a step toward shining bright like a galactic superstar! Taking action immediately means that you must read on quickly to cover all the steps in finding your passion first with your "feelings," and then focusing on and understanding yourself with your "being" needs, so that you can make the right decision about your glory path ahead, darling. Hence, it's very crucial for you to soak up all the information like a cute little sponge before making the biggest decision toward your Shiny happy ending. It's especially very important for you to diagnose your current feelings together with the reasons behind them so that we can begin your galactic path with the knowledge on how to make you feel better and shinier, darling. I really want you to know your passion, find your passion or feel your passion with clarity and with certainty! That's the whole idea, my dear, to let your Shiny soul come alive by measuring your feelings.

And because your feelings are the language of your soul, by measuring your feelings we will be measuring your soul's happiness and fulfillment level, darling. ⭐ Don't you like that? Don't you like to have a scorecard about your fulfillment in your galactic life? I know you do! ⭐ Therefore, please have your articulate professional attitude on and read on!

Because I have another exercise for you to analyze your feelings in your galactic life, darling, and it's called *"the stardom of a galactic life"* exercise:

THE STARDOM OF A GALACTIC LIFE

Alright, Shiny, I want you to get a pen and a paper, sit tight and start measuring your life to find out whether it is shining like a galactic superstar or not.⭐ Because if it is, then your scorecard would be full of all 9s and 10s; and maybe even 8s, giving you the "STARDOM AWARD" in your galactic life, my dear darling. ⭐

Now, all you need to do is score the level of your feelings—your happiness and your fulfillment level—from 1 to 10, 1 being the lowest and 10 being the highest. When you are scoring your galactic life, please be brutally honest!

And before you do that, here is some information about each and every area for you to analyze:

1. Your Physical Life:

It's your bodily health, your vitality, and your energy level to get this done and move on in your life, along with the way you look and your esthetic fulfillment about the way you look. And this is your number one priority in your stardom performance, darling! Gotta set the foundation strong, so as not to go wrong! ⭐

2. Your Emotional Life:

Your emotional life is a combination of your emotional states that you experience on a daily basis, Shiny. And your emotional states are what we call "moods." Because at the end, life is time, time is days and days are moments, right? Think about it: Our only vehicle to experience our moments is the way we feel about them—our moods! For example, are you generally a happy person, 9 out of 10, or an upset person finding yourself resenting at other galactic beings 7 times out of 10? In other words, how

141

satisfied are you with your general emotional state of mind, darling?

3. Your Social Life:

Human beings are social creatures, my dear. They need each other both to step up with them and also to step down on them. It's just the way it is. Basically, the quality of your social life comes down to the quality of your relationships. Tell me: How are you doing with your relationships, honey?

4. Your Professional Life:

This one is tricky, darling. Because when I say "professional," I also mean the way you use your time, your mission in life and what you contribute to the world with what you are good at. You might as well be a housewife who loves designing jewelry or decorating tables or a non-profit volunteer. The point is how satisfied are you with the way you use your time.

5. Your Financial Life:

Some say, "Money cannot buy happiness," and some say, "Money is the happiness." Well, it's about what kind of a relationship you have with money and how satisfied are you when it comes to your finances and your material needs.

6. Your Spiritual Life:

I gotta admit, not every galactic being has a sense of spirituality, honey. But you, as a galactic leader, you understand the contribution and the celebration that your soul craves for. Even holding this Shiny book in your hand makes you an elevated, soul darling. So tell me how connected you feel to the power of this miraculous universe.

Now, go measure your galactic manifestation, dear doll!

1. Physical life   1 2 3 4 5 6 7 8 9 10
2. Emotional life   1 2 3 4 5 6 7 8 9 10
3. Social life   1 2 3 4 5 6 7 8 9 10
4. Professional life   1 2 3 4 5 6 7 8 9 10
5. Financial life   1 2 3 4 5 6 7 8 9 10
6. Spiritual life   1 2 3 4 5 6 7 8 9 10

How did it go? Did you get the Stardom award, honey?

YOU ARE A STAR!
GET YOUR
STARDOM ON

Or did you see some horrifying results from your galactic feelings? I hope not! Because, once again, galactic leaders are born to live with passion, not with tension, darling.

However, if for some reason, your scores are not reflecting your passion, then keep calm, read on and get ready to get your stardom on.☆

Because I have another galactic law that will simplify your thinking process along the way, my dear Shiny, and it's a really good one:

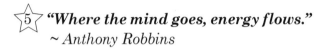

⟨5⟩ *"Where the mind goes, energy flows."*
~ *Anthony Robbins*

Listen, darling. You have the power of choosing what to focus on! Wanna see how?

<u>Let's do an exercise together:</u>

Go back to my first sentence above starting with "Listen" and tell me how many Rs you count in that sentence. Quickly! Done? OK, now tell me how many. If you counted only two Rs, you got it right, honey. Congrats! But that's not the point. ⭐ The point is that you don't know how many Os were there because you were focusing on the Rs. Get it? You will only see, hear or feel what you focus on, weeding through anything else that's out there available for your experience! Still yet, by the power of your own focus, and your selective attention, you will only see what you have previously decided to see, honey.⭐

What's more, by focusing on a specific angle (just like you focused on the Rs above) that you have subconsciously decided, you will start to perceive what you see as your reality or your perspective in life by collecting information about what you keep your focus on. For example, if you keep your focus on how beautiful the trees are while you are driving and keep staring at the trees, you will not notice the names of the streets as you pass them. If only you consciously and intentionally focus on the names of the streets, then you will decide to look at them and eventually see them.

And guess what? Just like you focusing on the Rs, another human being might as well be focusing on the letter U! Therefore, he doesn't get to see what you see in your own galactic reality. He gets to see his own and lives inside his own. And the funny thing is you both "assume" there is only life, one reality and one truth in our galaxy!

Oh, my gosh! Isn't that a BIG FAT ENLIGHTENMENT, sparkly? Isn't that amazing to realize the power of your own focus? Think about it deeply and thoroughly. The truth of the matter is that the number of existing realities are the same as the number of galactic beings, my dear, since we all have our own! Does that make sense, Shiny? I know it does. And I know you are slowly beginning to pick up the galactic laws that are governing our breathtakingly wonderful universe.

So, keep on picking it all up, and let's take a look at this magical power of our focus here.

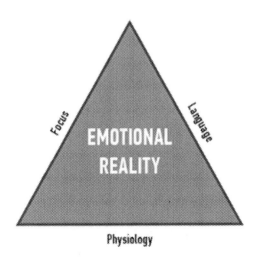

As we said, one of our galactic rules is, "*Where the mind goes energy flows.*" And just by looking at this diagram above, you will understand where it is coming from, dear.

Your FOCUS is one of the components of your very own emotional reality, my darling. How?

Well, let's do another exercise for you to see that:

Do you remember the very first time you kissed someone, or held hands or even kept staring at each other? How young were you back then? How did you feel? Who was that very first galactic creature that shared this experience with you?

If you genuinely let your sparkly brain wonder deep into the years in your mind—and of course if you had such an experience—you already dove into the emotional storage of this past experience by now, maybe sighing, maybe smiling. 🌟 Because first you simply focused on it, and by reading my questions you started an internal dialog with your own past experiences in your Shiny head, and with the help of the language you used to yourself, you were able to get more detailed information about that specific incidence, resulting in the creation of this emotional reality that you are feeling right here, right now. The incidence is about the past, it is not happening right here, right now, but because you were able to use the power of your focus, you were able to feel the feelings you felt before.

How is that for a change, Shiny? You see, you have the power to change the way you feel instantly and intentionally! Instantly darling, I am truly hoping to see the shocking look on your glowing face, because this stuff you are learning right now is mind-blowing!

So, at this point, you can practice using your focus effectively and powerfully, dear. 🌟

YOU ARE A STAR!
FOCUS ON
PRIORITIES

I am literally showing you how to instantly shift your focus from darkness to brightness and from nonsense to your own sense so that your whole being starts shimmering, my darling. Because:

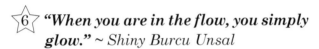

6 *"When you are in the flow, you simply glow."* ~ *Shiny Burcu Unsal*

This sixth galactic rule is from your Queen B now. What my rule implies is that when you feel absolutely and amazingly alive, aligned with your purpose, on a sacred path with your passion pounding in your heart, your actions fulfilling your soul, it means that you are in the flow. And when you are in the flow, because every inch of your body and every cell of yours dances with this flow, from head to toe, you start to glow.

Listen Shiny, your body has wisdom sweetheart. The wisdom of your Shiny happy feelings and not so Shiny or happy feelings are all stored somewhere in your body. Where do you think your emotions are coming from? You didn't think that they just appeared out of the Shiny blue sky, in the heat of the moment, did you? Oh, my darling, just kidding.

An emotion is a physiological state that is evoked by a stimulus like your own thought, or any other input from your outside world, honey. And a feeling is the end product of these evoked emotions. Well I am deliberately saying "evoked" because emotions are not really created in the heat of the moment, sweetheart. They have come a long way from millions of years of evolution, so that you feel them, get to know them, give language to them and use them to your benefit in your Shiny success path.

And we do have a cool technique that is called *"kinesiology"* to consult to your body when you need the certainty about your emotions. For example the certainty of what you will be doing to let your power shine out in your galactic path, because you have some alternative routes that you can choose and they all kinda feel good for you. And that's why you want to consult the wisdom of your body to choose the one with the strongest existence among them as an emotional resource. Wanna see how?

1) OK, the first thing you need is somebody else with you in this exercise. Because they will be doing the muscle test for you. So go get somebody!

2) Ask that person to push your left arm (if feels fatigue you can use the other arm, as well) down at step 4, 5, 6 and 7.

3) Stand up, take a deep breath, raise your left arm at your shoulder level and think about your name. Maybe the letters on your ID and how it sounds when somebody calls you and the certainty of knowing your name.

4) Say your name out loud by focusing on one spot and resist to the person pushing your left arm down.

How did it feel? Strong as steel, I know. ⭐ That's how certain your body feels about your name, naturally. ⭐ You know why, darling? Because you have heard your name for your age of years and you have written it everywhere, told it to everyone and repeated it over and over again. So your name existed with you as long you existed, creating a very thick neuro-muscle in your mind, easily communicating and transferring this knowledge to the muscles of your arms! Isn't that incredible?

Think of it as if all the cells in your beautiful body are chanting your name all together, like an army marching in a perfect harmony, eventually creating that full force of congruence feeling that your muscles stand up for. This is sharpness Shiny! This is the kind of knowledge that will keep you away from your false evidences appearing real (FEAR) and take you to the places you have never been! This is bliss, Shiny! This is the kind of a bliss that all the galactic leaders long for. And this is where we are going together in this book, sweetheart! ⭐

So get ready to shine the sharpness of your edges, baby!

5) Now, go back to staying erect and raise your left arm again, parallel to the floor by saying what you want in #1 out loud.

How did it feel? Did you feel the same strength as you felt with your name? Is it very close to it? If so, this is a great sign! The intelligence of your neurons is yelling to you that this is a great choice Shiny! Your body feels the existence of your choice already deep inside! Isn't that amazing?

But if, for some reason, your arm went down, then go to the next step and test another choice my dear.

6) Go back to staying erect and raise your left arm again, parallel to the floor by saying what you want in #2 out loud.

How did it feel now? Stronger or weaker compare to your want #1? You are already loving this test, aren't you?⭐ I almost see the smile on your face, Shiny. Next!

7) Go back to staying erect and raise your left arm again, parallel to the floor by saying what you want #3 out loud.

Well, by now you should have your clarity about which path to follow to shine, right darling? And it was that easy to measure your feelings, honey! Congratulations on becoming clear about your Shiny path ahead! ⭐

YOU ARE A STAR!
FEEL GOOD

7 *"Who you surround yourself with is who you eventually become."* ~ Anthony Robbins

Oh, darling, look around and tell me who do you see around you? And please don't tell me that you are surrounded by negatively programmed, limitedly operating and barely surviving robotic beings! Please don't! If for some reason, that's the case, just RUN! I kid you not, sweetheart! You have no idea what kind of damage you are doing to yourself! And, no it doesn't matter who they are! And no it doesn't matter if they are good people with good intentions, either! What matters is what happens to you at the end, and I know that it's not something that you would enjoy if you and I had psychoanalysis about the damage it did to your mind. Remember, sparkly, in every action there is a positive intention. So of course they are good people with good intentions. But their intention might be good only for themselves and not you! How about the Galactic Leader's Fulfillment Theory, darling? Don't you see that we human beings are created to receive, rather than to give? So they are in it to win it, as well, just like you! Whatever it is that they are trying to win out of hanging out with you! Maybe just sureness, maybe your acceptance, or a little indifference as they are bored to the heavens of this planet, due to a constant complaining award they have given to themselves? Who knows? And what do you get out of it? Learning to focus on negativity? Learning how to feel bad in any given moment? And, most importantly, learning why not to hang around these types of beings for your galactic shine's sake? Right?

And there are other types of people that, once you are exposed to their mind maps, their productivity and their fulfilment styles, you instantly detect the galactic power shining through their lives. And that's where you wanna hang around, my dear darling. You wanna position yourself around the big players, who are rocking their galactic worlds with self-regulation, motivation, discipline, belief and action! You wanna be around REAL, fascinating, mind blowing galactic leaders, to be like them, my darling!

So, if I ask you to choose between hanging out with those "close" friends of yours for spending your time in complaining about life, people, things and situations and meticulously discussing the specific reasons of why they suck or life sucks and things of that nature, doing nothing productive, uplifting or energizing, vs. investing your time, your energy and your mind in understanding the mental strengths, learning galactic success strategies and aiming to generate the magnetic energies of those high achievers in your life, which one would you go with, Shiny? Which one sounds more appealing to your galactic being, darling?

YOU ARE A STAR!
CHOOSE SMART

⭐8 ***"You may not have the resources that you need, but you will always have the resourcefulness if you seed."*** ~ *Shiny Burcu Unsal*

In life, there will be obstacles. That's the meaning of life, to go over the challenges, make progress and feel more confident and more fulfilled about yourself. And this eigth Galactic Rule will remind you a very simple yet frequently forgotten truth about your galactic power inside: The power of resourcefulness!

Yes, you have goals, you have desires and you have ambition in life to achieve great things. Yet you feel stuck because you say to yourself that you don't have the right ingredients for you to bake the success cake in your life. Because if it's really about the cake, then all you need to do is to go get the right ingredients for your success cake. Not to sit at home and feel sorry that you don't have the ingredients, right, Shiny? When it comes to creating the results you really want in your galactic path, it is never about the resources, it is the resourcefulness darling!

And that mentality, that resourceful thinking strategy, is what will separate you from the rest of the crowd, honey. You may not have the resources you need, but you will always have the resourcefulness if you seed. Yes, you have to seed the resourcefulness in you so it grows and materializes itself outside of you. You have to have that thinking, embedded in the thousands of miles of vessels in your brain, so that it becomes a habit of your neurons. You literally are a byproduct of your neurons upstairs! And it is your job to teach them how to be resourceful.

Let me give you an example. When you were a cute little stardust and wanted to become a successful doctor, you went ahead and studied the medical science, anatomy, chemistry, biology, etc., whatever you needed to learn to become a doctor, right? Or if you wanted to become an actor, a hairdresser, a movie director, a singer, a real estate broker, a pianist, a lawyer, a pharmacist or a dentist—you name it—whatever it was you wanted to become, what did you do first? You studied how to become that person you wanted to become, right? Well, I call it collecting the resources even though you didn't have them all to start with. But you wanted to become that person so much so that you dedicated yourself to it and acted resourceful about it and gathered all the resources you needed. That's how you do anything in life! No different than baking your success cake, isn't it?

Then what is it stopping you right now? If you claim that you don't have the resources, all you do need to have is your resourcefulness, darling!

YOU ARE A STAR!

BE
RESOURCEFUL

⭐9 *"Definition of insanity: Doing the same thing over and over again and expecting different results." ~ Albert Einstein*

You know, Shiny, a galactic leader is born to think out of the box, because she doesn't live in a box to begin with! Caged living is not for beings with galactic nature. You should know better, darling. Galactic leaders lead their own galaxy with their body-mind-soul power within! And that, my friend, requires some galactic thinking. Albert Einstein once touched based of the definition of insanity. Why do you think so? Well, darling, he is Einstein; he has the mind of a million galactic years of worth! He formulated the quantum theory and related that to our cosmic history. How do you feel about that? Definitely galactic leader material!

It was his passion to study the math behind the physical world, and that physical science required some real, galactic thinking, my darling. And when he was pondering on his mind-blowing ideas, he discovered that he had to come up with another approach when things didn't work out. He discovered that the same level of thinking we used when we were creating the problem wouldn't really be the answer to solve the same problem. He had to go out of his original thinking. And then he created his legendary definition of insanity: Doing the same thing over and over again and expecting different results! Does that something familiar to you? I hope not, darling.

As a galactic leader, it's a major requirement that you have flexibility in your behaviors, darling. It's a big major galactic rule that you don't always do the same thing and expect different results in your life. Just have it as a technique, and whenever you realize you are desperately repeating yourself and still not getting the result you want, change your thinking right away. Get a new approach, see the situation with different glasses, change your focus, change your language or change your environment.

Let's say that you are working on a project for hours and you feel like you are bored and it has taken its toll on you. You are forcing yourself to stay seated and stay focused. However, you are not able to think clearly or creatively or write easily. At that moment, you need to realize that you must do something different. You might get up, take a walk, wash your face, drink a cup of tea, listen to your favorite song, call a friend, watch a YouTube video—whatever it is that will be different from whatever you have been doing, you must do that to gain your focus back.

By the same token, if you want to have something you have never had before, you must first do something you have never done before. You just can't expect the universe to send you magical powers to get the results you want, honey. You must work hard on your results. You must first program your mind, your focus and your beliefs, and then change your actions as needed to create the results you want from your galactic life.

As a result, you must always start with the right kind of thinking in your head, darling. Always!

Well then, how are you going to have the right kind of thinking, huh? Good question! Because the right kind of thinking is only about asking the right kind of questions, my darling. Let's do an exercise together to find out what kind of thinking you have in your mind. When you are ready, grab your pen and paper and answer my question below:

Q: If you are going through a big challenge in your life, which questions do you usually end up asking yourself?

a) Why the bad things keep happening to me?
b) Why am I always unlucky and unsuccessful?
c) Will I ever have a happy life?
d) How stupider could I ever be?
e) What can I learn from what I am experiencing and what can I do differently to get better results in this situation?

Well, Shiny, it's kind of expected for you to not only ask but also master the e type of questioning skill to shine your galactic path, darling. As you clearly see, the questions a, b, c and d above are not going to produce any kind of positive, proactive or pragmatic answers that you could use in your life. These are obviously not the right kind of thinking and not the right kind of questioning.

A galactic leader is a doer. With the take-aways from her experiences, she builds up an army of proactive knowledge. The knowledge upon which she can do galactic magic. A doer has creative skills. And creative skills come from productive, proactive, resourceful thinking. And that's the reason why you have to have the right kind of skills before you decide to do anything in your galactic path, darling.

YOU ARE A STAR!

THINK DIFFERENT

As for learning new skills, that's not a secret that no one will ever tell. Here is how:

10 *"The queen of any of your beloved skill is the repetition, my dear."* ~ *Shiny Burcu Unsal*

I can go ahead and give you a countless numbers of galactic rules to Be-Live, to live and apply, my darling, but I am determined to **K**eep **I**t **S**imple and **S**exy (KISS) for you. So here comes the final rule of your galactic being: The queen of any of your beloved skill is the repetition my dear. Repetition, repetition, repetition!

Do you remember the first time you ever talked, walked even get shocked? You did them all by repetition. You learned each and every of them in time, by doing it over and over again, until how to do it finally stuck to your head, right? Did you know how to read, how to write or how to do math before going to school? Ok, don't start telling me you were one of those "clever" ones who learned how to read before school, because it doesn't matter when you learned it or where you learned it, what matters is HOW you learned it, darling! You learned by repetition! So there you have it! The secret behind any kind of a skill is a carefully practiced doing! You gotta do it over and over again to master it, darling! That's what a galactic leader does—she masters her stardom skills and she shines! ⭐

YOU ARE A STAR!
HAVE SKILLS

Now, my starshine, we are going to start up with designing your galactic path. For that, I want you to be in your best mood, *por favor*. So take the deepest breath ever to fill your cells with the vibrant feeling of the oxygen and let go. Take another one deeply, and slowly let it go…. When you are ready, you can begin to relax all your muscles in your body, starting from the ones on your forehead, going down to your chicks, the muscles around your mouth and now your shoulders, your elbows, your stomach, your knees and eventually your toes…. When you are ready to let go, just BE in the now with me.

Imagine you are the brightest galactic STAR in the whole universe with the most amazing, dazzling and mesmerizing feeling you create on the people who stare at you! Imagine your Shiny sharpie edges are your wings and your wings are your magic machines that make you travel in time! You have the power to go back to the beginning of time or to go forward till the end of time! Imagine you are the only one who can do that; no other living creature can possibly do what you can do. And because of this very reason, you owe it to your playmates here on earth to travel back and forth to collect the most advanced technologies of the human mind in the whole universe, so that we can all learn from you and use our minds a lot more effectively and powerfully and resolve fully to be and stay happy!⭐ This is your mission—to enlighten all the minds of humanity on earth as the brightest galactic star in the sky, darling. How would you fulfill this mission and where would you start?

You would first go find the most advanced mind technologies in time as your resources and then compare them with what we know today as mind technologies and eventually fill the gap with what we do not know, right, my Shiny head?

Well, if you would do it this way, congratulations! You are really advanced in your mind technologies. ⭐ But if you don't, then let's talk about this a little bit. Let's say that you would start by analyzing our current resources, i.e., what we know today about the mind technologies, and then go travel into the future to compare what we know today with what we will know tomorrow. Don't you think that your existing information will create a bias for you? Don't you think that that bias will eventually become a burden on your own mission of collecting technologies? Neurologically speaking, it is similar to the reason why we procrastinate—being "stuck" in the present state of mind, instead of being driven by the desired state of mind. Allow me to explain how.

The human mind works in a specific hierarchy of neurological processes that we call "*META MODEL*" in NLP language. Meta Model simply is the computation process of our brains when the information enters inside. As you already know by now, the new information can only enter into our personal computers upstairs through our five (VAKOG) senses. And when there is new entry, the following processes take place, as you will see from the diagram below:

1) Comparison
2) Deletion
3) Distortion
4) Generalization
5) Assumption

NLP COMMUNICATION MODEL

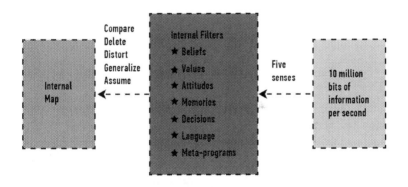

Comparison: *"Which one do you like more, the lychee or the passion fruit, darling?"* This is an obvious example of our "comparison" process up in our heads. But how about: *"A new intelligence theory was proposed by Howard Gardner in 1983 that differentiates it into specific (primarily sensory) **modalities**, rather than seeing intelligence as dominated by a single general ability. What do you think about his new theory?"* Well, this question requires you to have existing knowledge in your head about the earlier intelligence theories, at least one of them, so that you can compare the two with each other, and analyze the pros and cons for both so that you can form your point of view about the new theory, right? In other words, this new information about "intelligence" needs to be processed in compare to your existing information on its way to being filed in your "intelligence" folder in your personal computer.

Or, more simply, what happens when you meet someone new? The moment you shake hands and you look them in the eye, your brain automatically scans this "new information" as a new person and tries to give it a meaning by sorting through the existing information in your folders, if that person matches your folders of male, female, young, old, smart, friendly, cool, funny, etc., by simply comparing him or her with your already existing folders in your brain. Does that make sense, my lovely Shiny? So the important thing here is HOW you create any of these folders of yours and HOW you label them. Because as you see they are your very own filters in life. They are the reason you see the world in different eyes from anyone else. They are your own unique software running constantly at the back of your brain; creating your map of reality as heaven or hell in any given moment of time.

For example, if you have a folder running as an automatic filter in your brain with the information "I don't trust people" in it, what do you think will happen when you meet a new person? Yes, you got it, sparkly head; your brain will automatically move this new person into the folder of "I don't trust people" and you will already be looking for clues why you shouldn't trust this person. Why? Because that is the software program you have in the head. It doesn't matter whether you created it consciously

or unconsciously! Where the mind goes energy flows—
remember, darling?

What to do then? Well, now that you know how
your brain uses existing information to process the new
information, it is your responsibility to find out what
conscious and unconscious programs you have running in
your computation process upstairs so that you can freely,
consciously and intelligently choose which ones to keep,
which ones to delete and which ones to change.

It is also critically important to use the *"comparison"*
technique in its most effective way so that your brain
learns how to *"not judge"* people, things, situations and
yourself because of the poor management of your neural
pathways.

Galactic leaders are the cosmic beings with this secret
knowledge, flexibility and ability to re-create any folders
in their heads so that they can enjoy a sustained level
of mental heaven in their life experiences. So watch out,
Shiny, you now have no excuses for your drama, because
you now know how to avoid pain and focus on your gain.

YOU ARE A STAR!

IT IS A
CURRICULUM
COMPARISON

Deletion: Your brain has a capacity to process 7+/-2
bits of information at any given time (you can google it as
Miller's Law, 1956). It is just how your brain works with
its average short-term memory, my dearest. Therefore,
it is natural that your brain automatically deletes a big

chunk of the information entering into it. My question is, what kind of information do you think is being deleted and why, sweetie pie?

Have you heard about the *"selective attention"* in psychology before? Your selective attention is what you consciously or unconsciously programmed your mind to focus on, my dear. Your focus can be on a need, on a want, on a goal or on a negatively structured self-sabotaging idea. And, yes, this selective attention of yours also becomes an automatic filter on your life experiences, on your actions and inactions, and on all kinds of behaviors, acting like the focus of your life camera, leaving everything else out! Wow! What enlightenment, right, Shiny? Can you imagine what have you been leaving out in life since you can focus only on limited things at any given time?

More importantly, where is your focus? Where is your conscious attention at? Are you paying attention to good things and awesomeness happening around you? Or have you mastered being a drama queen since you have been focusing on the reasons why you are not good enough and why life sucks and why you can never get out of your cage, my lovely Shiny?

It is time to pay attention to what you are paying attention to! It is time to see what you are looking at and hear what you are listening to so that you can freely, consciously and intelligently keep the ones that are good for you, leave the ones that are not good for you and change the ones that can later become great for you! Teach your brain what to focus on and what to delete my darling—this is how you do it! This is how you manage the automatic *"deletion"* process that's constantly going on upstairs in your brain!

Wondering how galactic leaders are managing their *"deletion,"* my dear? They delete the excuses, the hardship, the limits and the reasons why not to go on with what they want and they happily choose to focus on their biggest reasons, their strongest talents, their most incredible power to overcome any challenges, and the mission of their lives as their purpose to go get what they want!

That's what a galactic leader does; she keeps calm and deletes the unnecessary on her way to shine her galactic path! So keep calm and delete on, my darling!

Distortion: You know sometimes you rush into arguments when people tell you what you did was wrong (*within the context of that specific situation*) and you automatically generate counter arguments—valid, tangible reasons why what you did was right—simply because you want to be "right," even though you know deep down that you were not? ⭐ Well, that automatic process of yours—to be able to generate counter arguments and all those valid reasons for your behavior instantly and consistently—is what we call *"distortion,"* my darling. ⭐ It is your brain's unbelievable ability to distort any kind of information at any given time for any kind of reason you want! ⭐

What happens is that your brain simply collects relevant data from all kinds of sources for you to feel safe and sound, which is associated with "being right" at that moment, because, if you remember, it is all about your survival, darling. The part of your brain that is responsible for your safety and security, your amygdala, has its very primitive 2 **F Functions** for you to survive in case of any kind of danger: **Fight** or **Flight**. With these very basic two options to gain pleasure and to avoid pain, your amygdala simply bypasses the thinking function of your evolved brain and triggers the fast, repeated and safe and sound option of automatic reactions.

Here is a paragraph on Amygdala's Fight-Flight Function from Harvard Medical School:

"This combination of reactions to stress is also known as the 'fight-or-flight' response because it evolved as a survival mechanism, enabling people and other mammals to react quickly to life-threatening situations. The carefully orchestrated yet near-instantaneous sequence of hormonal changes and physiological responses helps someone to fight the threat off or flee to safety. Unfortunately, the body can also overreact to stressors that are not life-threatening, such as traffic jams, work pressure, and family difficulties." http://www.health.harvard.edu/ newsletters/Harvard Mental Health Letter/2011/ March/understanding-the-stress-response

As a summary, if you are not <u>consciously</u> choosing your own actions and reactions in life, whatever you are automatically doing with your thoughts, language and behaviors in times of unpleasant situations is basically your primitive ability to distort the threatening situations so that you can find safety and feel the comfort, my darling. ⭐ So it is time to get civilized and control your primitive impulses, my dear Shiny!

A O S, it looks like you have just gotten enlightened!!! ⭐ Keep calm and distort your unconscious reality! ⭐

Generalization: Well, well, well.... Here we are, talking about the filing process of your Shiny brain, my galactic leader. Are you ready to dive in to the fourth automatic process of your brain, my darling?

Then, let's start with an example! Please fill in the blanks:

My best friend is_____

Red means_____

Money is_____

If you answered "myself," "passion" and "power" in order, you are right! Just kidding!⭐ Of course there is no right or wrong answers, my dazzling Shiny. You already know it, don't you, my darling? ⭐ My point is for you take a look at your answers and realize how "general" they are! Haven't you ever felt like friendship, the color red or money can mean something else for you? Depending on the situation, my dear? Well, here we are, highlighting the importance of the *"context"* of any situation and therefore the importance of **Contextual Intelligence**!

Without the context, your Shiny galactic brain will do what it's wired to do! It will generalize all the information in your memory bank in one single meaning and reveal it when needed! Because, my sparky head, your brain is where you file your life information as experiences, beliefs, values, goals, funny moments, sad moments, happy moments, etc., so that you can have your own "meaning," your own map of reality.

It is great that we have this automatic functioning of "generalization" so that the information filed upstairs can protect from dangers and help maintain safety and security, my dear. It's all survival. Again! ⭐

So, what to do with it? Simply be aware and manage it effectively according to the context of any given situation. How to analyze the context? Well, you got it, my Shiny! Remember the 6W+1H technique, my darling? That's exactly what you need to use in your everyday galactic experiences, so that you refrain from filing (generalizing) the two different kinds of information into the same folder and are able to have "distinctions" in life.

For example, if somebody—it can be your very best friend, too, my dear—tells you that there is something wrong with you because you keep changing jobs every two years, don't buy into that statement right away, my cutie. First analyze! Ask yourself these questions:

6W+1H CONTEXT COMPONENTS:

What is it that is bugging you that you want to change your job?

When exactly is it happening? Before or after certain feelings or certain food, etc.?

Where is it about? A specific company, a specific industry or a specific city?

What resource dictates that there is something wrong with changing jobs every two years?

Why do you feel like you need a change? What is your intention behind?

Who is it that is making you feel you want to quit your job?

How do you change jobs? What is your communication and behavior style when you leave?

When you ask these questions and get your own distinctive answers about your own communication and behavior patterns you will turn on the lights, my darling. There won't be any more darkness in your world because you will KNOW why you are doing something and how to do it in the most effective way, my dear!

It might be a specific behavior of a specific person, or a specific industry that is not true to your identity, that is causing your soul to roar, my dear. Or it might be a specific time of the day that your body releases certain stress hormones that you need to be aware of, my darling. You might as well be on a mission to let your power shine out but you might need a little more persistence, consistence and confidence about your reality.

And with this knowledge and enlightenment, you will no longer buy into the arguments and opinions of others and protect your confidence. You will no longer Be-Live in other's headlines, my dear! You will create your own!!! You will have your own reasons and your own purpose to rise above any challenges your soul faces so that you can shine like a bright galactic leader, my dear!⭐ And the best thing is that you will also go ahead and make your galactic friends SHINE bright like galactic leaders, as well, my darling!⭐ This is how we are all going to end the ugly darkness in the world and bring the Star shine in!!! ⭐ Isn't that exciting, my darling?⭐

YOU ARE A STAR!
DON'T BE-LIVE
THE HEADLINES

Assumption: After all that comparison, deletion, distortion and generalization happening in your head, of course what you have in your mind is not the reality, but only the perception of the reality, my darling. Which is basically your "assumption." Makes sense, right? Think about 7 billion people in the world with their limitless amount of experiences, beliefs, thoughts and values.... Whose opinion is right? Who has the answer for everything? Who is the best resource for reality?

YOU, my Shiny! YOU and YOU! And if there are already 3 million people reading this book, which means there are 3 million of YOU, who is right? Tell me!

Get it? YEAH!!! You got it, my sparky head! Everybody is right! And everybody has her own reality! Because everybody has her own information processed and filtered through her own experiences, beliefs, values, goals, etc.! And that makes everybody right! Within their own context of course!

Well, that's exactly why NLP looks at people and their behaviors separately, my lovely. Because people might be good or even great with diamond hearts. But if their behavior sucks, the chances are they won't be perceived as "good" people. This is just another generalization your galactic head does, my darling. Putting people and their behaviors in the same category. Oh, no! Not at all!

Think about it, just because you couldn't remember the name of a person once, are you a person with bad memory? Or just because an awarded chef messes up the food just once simply because he forgot it in the oven, is he a bad chef? No! These are occasional situations, under the necessity of one's contextual intelligence to measure the conditions and the framework of that specific behavior. These are not the attributes of these people!

So please, my dear Shiny, it is your great responsibility as a galactic leader to separate people from their behaviors. It is also your great responsibility to apply your contextual intelligence in any given situation so that you can come up with the healthiest measurement of that specific situation my dear. Allright?

Well, then, how do we decide what's the best behavior, right? How to measure a behavior to start with? Do you remember? We covered this part before in Chapter 2, my lovely Shiny. Please refer to the Principle of Behavior in Universal Principles of the Mind on page 37. A galactic leader is the one who can freely choose and deliberately demonstrate **A Class** behaviors in her Shiny galactic path, my darling. ☆

YOU ARE A STAR!
BEHAVE LIKE
A LADY

WE ARE NOT HERE TO TAKE OR HAVE.
WE ARE HERE TO GIVE AND BE.

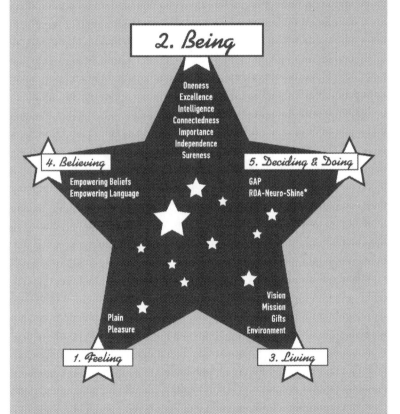

2. BEING

Well, now that you are all clear about your feelings and how important your feelings are to you, my dear Shiny, we can now move on to analyzing your galactic being as your second step into shining your galactic path ahead. This is our second step before making any neural connections that we call "decisions" that will shape your destiny, honey. You will be diving into the study of your own being, along with the psychological reasons behind each and every thing you do, darling. So, are you ready to unleash some fulfillment theory about your Shiny self? Then, listen up, sweetheart!

YOU ARE A STAR!
LISTEN UP

Galactic leaders are not that grounded, as they are born to fly in the sky. Yet, even these spirits of excellence have their own galactic desires to be fulfilled level by level, as they are a part of the universe of beings. Do you know which of your humanly wants and needs you are trying to fulfill with what you do, Shiny? Or better yet, do you really know what your real motivations are, sweetie? Because, my dear, behind every galactic action of yours, there is a positive intention. ⭐

It's absolutely true that sometimes we are carried away with the things that we want instead of what we need. It is almost like trying to calm a crying baby with ridiculous faces and gestures, hoping to distract her mind from whatever she is focusing on, when what she really needs is a fresh new diaper.⭐. In other words, you might as well distract your Shiny self from whatever the need you really need by shifting your consciousness and your focus to some other wants or needs. However, you should know that you are no different than a baby, my darling. ⭐ So, you won't stop needing or wanting it just because you are busy trying to achieve some other things.⭐ The GAP will still be there, inside of your cosmic system, darling, eventually making you fall back to your initial motivation, until that one gets fulfilled. This is the main reason why so many other beings, like the physical or the transit beings do not feel totally fulfilled; they are trying to fulfill the *"wrong"* want or need—the GAP that they can reach at the surface level, not the real, deep GAP they need to dig deep to reach at—and therefore are not achieving successful, long-lasting results.

And that's exactly why it's our job as galactic leaders, to differentiate our needs from our wants as our deep motivations in anything we do, my darling. Because the distinction between the two might mean the whole world for you or, better said, the whole universe for you. ⭐ Think about it. What is a need and what is a want? What makes them different from each other? And what are you really trying to achieve when you do what you do? What is the real GAP are you trying to fulfill, my Shiny? Let's explore!

If you feel hungry, for example, assuming that you are healthy, fit and not on a special diet, just any type of "food" is what you really need as a fuel for your system and as a charge for your body, functionally and operationally. But the *"kind of food"* that you choose with your conscious decision would be what you want among the options you have at that given time ⭐ In other words, the distinction between a need and a want is such a thin line that it is very easy to miss. And one can argue both depending on the circumstances. Plus, it is your God-given, cosmic nervous system and your socially shaped neural pathways that can turn a want into a need for you in the blink of an eye, my Shiny darling. Oh, yes, they can, honey! ⭐ Watch and listen to this:

Not long ago, just about 20 years ago, did you know what an iPhone was? Or what a mobile phone was, to start with? Probably not. ⭐ Well then, how come it has become a need for the 98 percent of the whole globe in our today's time? You may answer, *"That's different because it is technology and it improves in time,"* but your human system also is and has its own operational technology that also improves in time, my darling. And that's why it adapts itself to situations and developments of the cosmic clock and with every new data entry to the galactic mind; a new want emerges in the system until it fulfills itself as a need of the time's being.

Just like your needs keep changing and changing and changing in time. ⭐

177

These are the seven levels of #**motivations** that even a galactic leader like you seeks to fulfill in her galactic path, my darling:

1) Acceptance & Comfort & Sureness
2) Difference & Independence
3) Specialness & Importance
4) Love & Connectedness
5) Curiosity & Intelligence
6) Identity & Excellence
7) Spirituality & Oneness

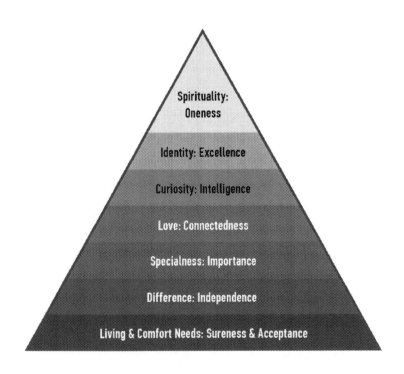

Galactic Leader's Fulfillment Theory

So let's take a closer look at this fulfilment theory of yours: ☆

1. Living & Comfort Needs: Sureness & Acceptance

My dear Shiny, you know that being alive/living is the very core of your galactic being. After all, you are one big, glamorous star with every inch of your existence. So it is an existential law that you have to turn your lights on first if you are going to shine on others. Think about it. How are you going to light up the rooms you enter in if there is a power shortage going on in your own system, my dear? ☆

Yes, you got me, babe. First, you gotta <u>make sure</u> that you are alive, safe and sound with a certain level of physiological <u>comfort</u> and a certain state of mind to <u>accept</u> who you are, how you are, where you are and with whom you are, etc., so that you can function properly in your path, darling.

Your **Living Needs** are your functional, operational, i.e., your basic survival needs, honey. As simple as oxygen, foods, bodily functions, a place to live like a shelter or a home, and being healthy. These needs are your number one priority in your galactic existence, darling, since you cannot fly without being charged with the nutritional fuel your body needs. Just like a car needing gas, your body needs oxygen, food and physical body maintenance needs to function and to #move forward in life.

Comfort Needs, on the other hand, are a little bit more than just living needs, sweetheart. You know how you feel the comfort of being in your warm bed in the mornings with every cell of your being and you don't wanna do anything but stay in that comfort zone? OK, that's the state of mind I am talking about. Your comfort is what your system longs for in your galactic space, I know. And I also know that the greatest achievements of all times have all taken place at the end of the comfort zones, honey. So you really must have the self-discipline to manage the level of your comfort so that you can get things done, my dear. If you keep focusing on the comfort of what you have now, you will never get a chance to taste the comfort of what else you could have had in the future, right? So in a way, by trying to stay away from any possible danger, you are also staying away from any available growth, excellence and prosperity in your path darling. Just remember to calculate the worth of your current comfort against the worth of possible other gains, sweetheart.

I know that there is a huge irony and an incredible contradiction but that's exactly how we are all wired as human beings, darling. What happens when you are too comfortable living in your house doing nothing and just enjoying the fulfillment of your comfort for days, for weeks? You get bored, right? Now you want to interrupt that comfort by doing something, anything different. Well, this is called "human nature," darling, welcome to the very shocking information about your cosmic nature, where "too much" of everything is not really fulfilling. ⭐ You don't need to go far to understand this nature of yours, baby. Just look at the nights and days and you will see the balance of the darkness and the light right there! Remember the cosmic law of correspondence? Just like that, my dear Shiny, we are also a combination of some darkness and some light. And, yes, it is up to your conscious decisions to choose one over another in your galactic journey, which I will cover in the next chapters, honey.

Sureness, at the very same physical being level is your need for certainty in your galactic life, my dear. From certainty of your existence to certainty of your ability to avoid pain and to gain pleasure, for most human beings, sureness means only survival. Well, we all need a sense of sureness that the roof above us and the floor below us will stay where they are! We all need to know that we are OK! As for galactic leaders like you and me, sureness means power, my dear! You know this already. ⭐ The power of knowing, the power of being and the power of mapping your path to shine bright like a magnificent galactic diamond! Sound familiar? And you want the sureness of that knowing.

Of course, the point here is how you use your power of being, my darling. In other words, what do you want to

181

make sure of in your Shiny path that can provide you with both acceptance and comfort at the very first level, dear?

You know some physical beings are really into making sure that they can control everything around them, including their households, working environments and even the behaviors of their friends! You cannot escape from their sureness weapons, my darling. They won't pass it, since it's their vehicle to meet their need for sureness. So be aware of this very basic motivation driving human behaviors, including yours!

Acceptance as a concept has a double meaning here. The first meaning is that you need to accept your own being with everything that comes with being you. ⭐ Your flaws and glows all together in the same existential basket! Why so? Because if you don't accept your own being, you can't survive, honey. You might even kill yourself or maybe even other beings if you are not somewhat OK with yourself! Yes, this ugly dark motivation is also built inside of us, darling! And, again, it's nothing but a conscious decision to do it or not to do it.

Or if you don't accept how things are or how other beings around you are, you cannot have a healthy, balanced mind free from negative thoughts, and eventually you cannot have peace in your life. Especially accepting yourself is key to your peace of mind here. Accepting your magnificent, cosmic experience in this physical world that we are in, with its glorious mountains and glamorous flowers in the nature, is the foundation for your galactic fulfillment, my dear Shiny.

But I need to make a clarification about what exactly I mean by accepting yourself, my darling, because we are talking about elevating our being to a galactic level with all that entails. And it does entail being fantastic with the way you show up in life, from the way you look to what you say and how you say it, to what you do and how you do it. And you may not have the critical thinking, effective communication and results-oriented, purposeful action strategies yet, or the professional, unique and "*something about her*" look that it takes to accept yourself as a galactic being, and it certainly, surely is a process of transformation. Get ready for it, my darling. Nobody is born with these skills but the ones with the biggest commitment are always rising to the top, my dearest.

So, it is very normal and expected that there will be changes and challenges you will face to become the version of yourself to the level of your acceptance as a galactic leader my dear. Everybody can talk, can walk and can look like a fantastic galactic leader, but not everybody will do it because it is not in our comfort zone. Get it? I am not saying that it's going to be easy to come even to the very basic level of accepting yourself as a galactic being, but it will absolutely be worth it, my Shiny! So, just keep calm and accept all the challenges. ⭐

YOU ARE A STAR!
ACCEPT ALL THE
CHALLENGES

The other meaning of **acceptance** is that you need to be accepted as who you are as a being by other beings around you or else you can't survive, either. For example, if you are a baby, your mommy needs to accept to have you in her life so that she can take care of you, feed you and comfort you, right? Or if you are a grown up, your parents or your partner or whomever you surround yourself with need to somewhat accept your being, otherwise your soul feels left out and you might harm yourself and harm others for that feeling of unacceptance, my dear. Trust me, you would. It's just the way we are emotionally wired up, darling.

Well, let's wrap it all up again. When you know that you survive and are alive safely, now you want the cushiony softness of your comfort zone. Sound familiar? ☆ Now you want to know which path is yours to draw your edgy shape on and which zones to comfortably carry on. Because it's time for securing your own shimmery zone and relaxing your galactic muscles with a nice deep breathe full of life. Oh, and not to mention the need for being accepted for who you are, with all the cracking sounds from your existence. Just simply existing is never enough for any human creature, including the galactic entities like you; there needs to be the acceptance, the approval of others at the second level, to co-exist happily ever after together. Isn't that right, Shiny? Spill it out, darling. It will be helpful just to remember and note the countless times that you hopelessly tried to be RIGHT about being you, right about existing and showing up in life as you, even though you knew that you weren't! This is the scary part, sweetheart, a very scary and very funny fact to dig in and ACCEPT.☆ Trust me, accepting your need for acceptance is only gonna make you a much more fascinating beauty to stare at. ☆

My question is, do you wanna be right or do you wanna get what you want, Shiny? Which one sounds more glamorous, sweetheart? How many times you felt weakened by your amygdala getting in charge and trying to control your emotions instead of your controlling your emotions? How many times have you let arguments prolong just to prove yourself right, even though you knew you weren't? Even knowing that you are not right, or may not be right, or better yet, understanding that everyone can be right depending on her own map of reality, you still just wanted to "WIN" in the heat of the moment. So you insisted and insisted at the cost of hurting that being in front of you and losing the opportunity that was available right before you, feeling less of yourself and costing you your peace of mind, your sureness and your emotional and psychological emptiness! It is insane how we do it, right? Yep! That's what I am talking about. ⭐

So, just fly SMART on your path and drop trying so hard to be right and choose to be smart and get what you want, honey!

YOU ARE A STAR!
YOU GET WHAT
YOU WANT

2. Difference: Independence

If you are ready, here comes your second existential motivation to fulfill, Shiny. This one is quite entertaining since it challenges your first need of securing your comfort. Who could have thought that with all the chaos, the challenges and the contradictions we experience in our lives we would be coming from the very psychology of our own built-in needs to fulfill? Because that's really all there is to it! Contradicting nature of human beings is the cause and the contradicting behaviors are the effects—just like your need to go out of your comfortable galactic zone and do, have and be something different from all the human beings, my superstar. ⭐ And that's what we call your very independence!

Everyone needs variety in her path. Everyone likes a little bit of a challenge; without it, life kinda sucks. ⭐ Can you imagine living a life by knowing everything? Knowing where to go when, what to do and how, how to do and why and why is it with whom? Oh, my. Even listening to it puts me into sleep. Dunno how you feel about it! Too much sureness and awareness would bore any kind of being on our planet, honey. We all need to be independent from everything we are dependent upon sometimes. ⭐ Here comes the contradiction again. ⭐ Can't escape it! It'll find you, chase you all over and eat you alive! ⭐ Because it's in our nature again. We feel most alive and fulfilled when we overcome challenges and surprises of an unwanted sort.

You know what, though? Gotta watch out again for a balance, Shiny! Because too much independence from the things you know will also make you way too much challenged and concerned. Think about it. You know that you can see your galaxy around when there is light around you. At night, if no light, no sight, honey! It's the same formulation. If no sureness, then doubt will kill you and kill all your unanswered questions before they begin.

So it's so important that you find your balance through your independence in your Shiny path and do it in the right way, honey. Because it's easy to be caught in the winds of change with the help of negative tools like excess alcohol and drugs to get the feeling of independence, and we don't want that! A galactic leader is a true leader because she can choose all her vehicles from positive sources!

Furthermore, you will need a certain amount of acceptance, comfort and sureness already going on in your galactic path so that you could appreciate a little difference and independence from them. Do you understand what I am saying, my dear? It's like going to Macy's and buying many shoes all at once to make yourself sure of your awesomeness, only after which you can go home and realize that you already had way too many Shiny high heels, and what you really needed was a pair of simple, black flat shoes to help assure your comfort on the road! Sound familiar, Shiny? You know, at the end of the day, I am here with my Shiny little book for you to get out of the darkness and to get into your sparkles, darling. ☆

YOU ARE A STAR!
SPARKLE ON

3. Specialness: Importance

Speaking of which, this will be no issue for you, because galactic leaders are born to be different than the crowd, or, better yet, be somebody more important! Sounds good, doesn't it, Shiny? Having edgier and sexier wings than other, regular, every day stars for a galactic leader like yourself sounds much more appealing, isn't that right, my darling? Oh, yeah, don't I know it!!! I do! Because it really doesn't matter if it's me, or you or anybody else, my dear; we all have it! We all wanna fly so high in the sky with the feeling of being somebody really important; and we all wanna shine so bright like a real, exclusive diamond!

But guess what? Too much specialty will taste like lonely planet, honey.  When you wanna fly so high and be so exclusive with your VIP status you kinda leave the rest behind and gradually disconnect from the crowd so that you end up wanting to re-connect. Isn't that ridiculously true, Shiny?

I know feeling different, a little distant from the rest is the original aim of fulfilling this need. However, things may change their color if you paint them too much with only one color, my darling. Look at your own colors! Don't you glare over others when you really, really shine so so bright? Yes, you do, right? Aha! That's what I am talking about, dear. Every now and then, you gotta keep it alright instead of making it too bright, just for the sake of belonging to your galaxy. You don't wanna imagine living in the endless darkness of lonely planet, I assume. That's the whole point, dear. Always leave 10 percent of your importance on the side and be bonafide.

YOU ARE A STAR!
BE BONAFIDE

4. Love: Connectedness

If not, you'll find yourself longing for feeling not so special and not so important, so much so that you will want to reconnect with the very same others that you didn't really want to connect with at all. Remember the contradicting psychology of your existential motivations, dear? If there is no balance, then there is no bill to pay, no matter financial or emotional. ⭐

Oh, Shiny, looks like you are deeply in love with your lovely self. ⭐ It's allright, darling. Enjoy every moment of true love, especially if you feel the deep connectedness at the divine level. Because some others are not as lucky as you are, my dear; they just wanna get away with a simple yet surface-level connection, instead of a frightening and discomforting feeling of commitment to love. And what's worse is they kinda call it "love," too. How dare are they, you're thinking? Correct? Nope, darling, nope! Drop that unaccepting thought, please. Remember your own first need for acceptance? Well, I have got news for you, my dear, you are not the only one with that need! The others want and need to be accepted, as well, even if they claim that they don't need to be! OK? Write that rule down as a fundamental source of your social shine and remember to let others be others, sweetheart. Because that's what they know with their own humanly experience and that's what they will have in their own comfort zone as "love" or whatever they name it. Just let go. I know you have that EGO, but let's drop the "E" and let "GO"! ⭐

Furthermore, if it makes them happy, your job would only be to shine on their happiness, my dear, not to shadow any sort of shininess, as you wouldn't welcome somebody else doing it to your heavenly feelings. Right, my dear? That's the way it goes in your galactic world, as well! Think about it, all the galaxies are spinning around their own existence and not letting each other shadow each other's shining zone. There is a respectful galactic space between you and your beloved ones up there! Isn't that right? So let's keep that space, for the sake of galactic level of love. OK, my galactic friend? 🌠

But for whatever the reason is, always, always Be-Live in TRUE LOVE darling! Love will heal you, elevate you, cherish you, change you and free you! Love is the answer to all the questions of our galactic beings. Love is where it all begins.

Think about your body, Shiny. Think about all those billions of cells in your body, co-existing happily and lovingly, with an infinite dignity and integrity for your wholeness. Your cells love each other, Be-Live it or not, unconditionally! If one of them hurts, the other will run up to help in a minute, always loving, always supporting. If another one does something wrong, many others will keep it calm and just carry on. Your body has the wisdom of GOD, Shiny! Your body understands TRUE LOVE, darling!

YOU ARE A STAR!
FIND TRUE LOVE

5. Curiosity: Intelligence

Curiosity killed the cat, but satisfaction brought it back! The satisfaction of knowing, learning, growing and expanding for a better version of your Shiny being; and the deepening for a bigger experience of your passionate living will keep you going in your shining path, darling. And this is the fifth level, which I call "Intelligence" in the hierarchy of your existential motivations, my dear. This is such a level that combines all the other ingredients from earlier stages and puts the cake in the oven to bake! This is the stage you get ready to rock and roll on your path my dear!

This is the stage that makes the difference in whether you make it in life. Because as you keep satisfying your curiosity with the new information, the different kind of knowledge about things in life and the intelligence you build from that self-esteem, you will quickly realize how much you didn't know about what you didn't know. That alone is a major breakthrough, my sweetheart! So this is a golden stage to be at! You see that? Then, go enjoy your intelligence and feel that!

YOU ARE A STAR!
STAY
INTELLIGENT

6. Identity: Excellence

It's not what you do in the endless, gorgeous sky with your marvelous wings to fly, or what you get from the sparkly universe; it's how Shiny you become that really matters, honey You know that every earthy being has a name, but not every being has an identity. And you also know that your identity is within reach of your own creativity. Go and get it!

Oh, Shiny! It seems like you now are at the level of ages of universal wisdom, darling. Don't you think that it's about time to declare your own identity and unleash your galactic creativity? Don't you see the levels you have climbed up to make it all the way up here? And don't you love it here? You know, my dearest, a great view is always seen from the top  So rise up! As they say, my lovely, if you want to feel up; you gotta dress up, show up and never give up! It's all for your excellence. All for your tangible, measurable and unforgettable strive for excellence, my galactic friend!

YOU ARE A STAR!

STRIVE FOR EXCELLENCE

7. Spirituality: Oneness

Then we finally arrive at our destination: Oneness with our Shiny happy universe!  You know Shiny, I Be-Live it's about time to reveal a very fascinating truth about your being, my dear. So sit tight now!

Remember I keep telling you that there is always a deeper level meaning, feeling and reasoning behind every single surface level behavior of us as galactic beings? Do you also remember that the deeper level of meaning and feeling is always the one we give to everything with the way we use our focus, language and physical body? Well then, connect the dots now, sweetheart! How come, do you think, you get to choose how to feel about anything that happens in your galactic path, darling? How come, do you think, the way you use your body can affect the way you feel about yourself, sparkly head? Think about it! I mean, really, truly, focus on each and every word I say here again! I am telling you that you get to be at the very emotional state you choose to be, regardless of what is happening, where it is happening, how it is happening and why it's happening. Plus, you get to change how you feel about it with the way you use your body! Could it be ever simpler than that?

Honey, all of us as galactic beings are spiritual beings having a physical experience on this planet! We are not at all physical beings having a spiritual experience, like you might have been thinking! OH, MY GOSH! Did you get it yet? Isn't that incredible to realize that?

Well, welcome to your top, cosmic motivation of spirituality, my dear Shiny. Because at this highest level of being, things are done at the highest level darling! Wondering why? Simply because galactic leaders are the highest level of galactic beings, darling, and they do have the highest sense of ONENESS with the universe as their reasoning, meaning and feeling behind everything that they do!

So, if you are claiming to be a galactic leader, darling, get ready to feel the heat of being at the top and deal the beat of leading from the top! ⭐

YOU ARE A STAR!
FEEL THE BEAT

Allright now, Shiny, now that you understand the fulfillment theory of a galactic leader, you must be jumping around in wonder. How you are doing in fulfilling your own galactic needs, right, my darling?

Then if you are ready, grab a fancy pen and paper and start measuring the way you fulfill your being needs in your current path, ranging from 1 to 10, 10 being the top. Oh, also, please notice that two of these needs are kinda your primary ones, darling. Choose your top two needs as well. And last but not least, think of your ways of getting them into your being, with both positive and negative ways.

1. How do you fulfill your need for acceptance, comfort and sureness in your life? *List some of the ways you try to make sure that you will have the comfort by avoiding pain and gaining pleasure?*

   -
   -
   -
   -

   How fulfilled are you for your need for acceptance, comfort and sureness in your life:

   1 2 3 4 5 6 7 8 9 10

2. How do you fulfill your need for difference and independence in your life? *List some of the ways you try to create independence, diversity and challenges in your life.*

   -
   -
   -
   -

How fulfilled are you for your need for difference and independence in your life:

1 2 3 4 5 6 7 8 9 10

3. How do you fulfill your need for feeling special and important in your life? *List some of the ways you try to be special, important and significant in your life.*

- -
- -
- -
- -

How fulfilled are you for your need for specialness and importance in your life:

1 2 3 4 5 6 7 8 9 10

4. How do you fulfill your need for connection and love in your life? *List some of the ways you try to feel love and connectedness in your life.*

- -
- -
- -
- -

How fulfilled are you for your need for love and connection in your life:

1 2 3 4 5 6 7 8 9 10

5. How do you fulfill your need for curiosity and intelligence in your life? *List some of the ways you try to be intelligent and grow your knowledge in your life.*

How fulfilled are you for your need for curiosity and intelligence in your life:

1 2 3 4 5 6 7 8 9 10

6. How do you fulfill your need for identity and excellence in your life? *List some of the ways you try to create your identity and be excellent in your life.*

How fulfilled are you for your need for identity and excellence in your life:

1 2 3 4 5 6 7 8 9 10

7. How do you fulfill your need for spirituality and oneness in your life? *List some of the ways you try to feel spiritual and be one with the universe in your life.*

How fulfilled are you for your need for spirituality and oneness in your life:

1 2 3 4 5 6 7 8 9 10

And here is the scoreboard for your enlightenment, honey. I want you to look at this scoreboard as a guideline for your growth.

SCORE	IDENTITY	BELIEF	MOOD
1	I am the victim	Life happens to me	Crisis
2	I am the victim	Life happens to me	Crisis
3	I am the victim	Life happens to me	Crisis
4	I am the victim	Life happens to me	Crisis
5	I am the fighter	Life happens to me	Aggresive, Controlling, Judgmental
6	I am the rationalizer	Life happens by me	Self-Concerning, No Integrity
7	I am the caregiver	Life happens by me	Drama, Sympaty for Others
8	I am the opportunist	Life happens through me	Personal Power, Synergy, Win-Win
9	I am the visionary	Life happens through me	Presence, Non-Judgemental, Risk Taker
10	I am the creator	Life happens as me	I am, Life is an Illusion, No Good or Bad

How are the results, Shiny? Does life happen to you, by you or through you?

Well, as you can guess, galactic beings are the ones at the top three, my lovely Shiny. Only the opportunists, the visionaries and the creators of this planet earth are qualified as **galactic leaders**. But before we go ahead and talk about all the amazing, mind-blowing and cosmic qualities of galactic leaders, let's start from the beginning and see what other beings reside in what other levels.

PHYSICAL BEINGS – in need of ENLIGHTENMENT

The first five levels are where all the **physical beings** of this planet reside, my dear. <u>These people do not question the **given life**.</u> They will be obedient in their caged circle. They will act and feel as if they have no voice or no choice in life. They simply are the effect of what others say or do or think or approve/disapprove of. They are so out of touch with their cosmic core that they literally live in a dark place, being in urgent need of enlightenment.

Many people live here, with their "*reaction mood on,*" either venting over their past and their incapacities, focusing on their limits in life in many different areas, and complaining about why "nobody understands them" or "why they can't do things" while others easily can. These physical beings almost feel trapped in their "given" identity and pre-framed destiny designed by some other people, some other things, their past or something else other than their own conscious and cosmic power within.

When you think about life in general, we all are enticed with carrots and sticks to do what others want or need us to do. We were all babies once, in need of parents or some sort of caregivers to teach us what to do, how to do it and why we need to do it in their given way, right? Think about it. How did you even start talking or walking? How did you learn that life was supposed to be in some certain way? You learned it from, and modelled the world of, your parents or caregivers who offered treats of acceptance, sureness, importance and love for your being, isn't that right? And it felt really comfortable to follow the rules of your given world since the external rewards, "carrots," better said, kept coming, I bet. They inevitably shaped your environment, your everyday behaviors and your skills you gained in life since you kept repeating the same behaviors over and over again—your values, your belief system, and eventually WHO you are in your core existence as a mere physical being.

Please, darling, don't you ever look at this statement as something to worry about. This place you live in only needs your AWARENESS to rise up to the next level. Because awareness is your only friend who can hold your hand in times of "reactive commands" from the primitive parts of your brain, hon. And how do I know that? Well, it's so easy to guess. Yes darling, I have been there and done it all at this "victim" mentality of physical beings. But I woke up! Thanks to the power of Neuro Linguistic Programming, I have seen what it was dark before. Just like the 70 percent of the dark matter in the universe. I discovered the darkness I was surrounded by. And I needed to rise up! I needed to fight for the level of life I wanted to live. I had to claim my own identity as a galactic leader and let my cosmic power shine out!

So you can do it, too! I know how to do it. ⭐ Great news! When I was trying to figure my way out, there were no other galactic beings who could guide me to my shining path of success and happiness. You are so lucky, my dear Shiny. You really are cosmically ready to rise up, the only thing it takes is to make your mind ready. And now that you are aware of a better way to live, are you willing to do the "hard *heart work*" that it requires for you to let your cosmic power shine out? If you are, just turn your mind on and read on! Or simply, come take my next live training at www.Be-Liveinu.com.

TRANSIT BEINGS – in need of EMPOWERMENT

Levels 6 and 7 are the ones in transition. They are not fully in the galactic realm of consciousness nor fully in the physical realm, so we call them the **transit beings**. They have traits and patterns from each side, still trying to figure out their path for empowerment, because they do question the given life with its given carrots and sticks. And that's how they were able to create a **comfortable** life: with questioning, with a different level of inner motivation to push the given boundaries and set their own. Haven't we all been there, enjoying how awesome the success feels, and how incredible being important is and how hard the "truth" seems? At the end of the day, we were able to differentiate ourselves from the crowded "physical beings" with their given lives, right? We were able to study hard and work hard in order to come to this point of respect by the society and success by the norms. But, unfortunately, we are still missing the richness of a galactic leader's fulfillment levels, still not even being close to those heightened levels of purpose and meaning, and still longing for the brighter colors, the deeper connections and the freer moments a galactic being happily lives.

Life at these levels feel not meaningless, obviously, but kinda mysterious, leaving you with tons of unanswered questions. You think you are having an OK, comfortable life, with the tangible and intangible assets you accomplished in life, like your career, your car, your house here and your house there, kids you raised, friends you have, etc. But something feels wrong, doesn't it? Something pushes you and bugs you inside. A voice in your head most probably saying, *"There is more. You can do more. How did I end up here to start with? Is that really what I want? Where did the ambition, my drive, go?"* And your life becomes a search in need of these answers, in need of more, in need of completeness.

But, of course, you have a pretty good functioning brain, used to comforting you with the counter thoughts like, *"Can't you just be satisfied with what you have got? You know how hard it was to get here. And you know how many would swap places with you! What else do you want? Just be grateful and get away with where you are and who you have become!"*

So you sit back. The gear of your life is one forward, one back, two forward, two back, leaving you hang in there with nothing less and nothing more. But the GAP you feel inside grows more. Oh, and another stopper is your environment, definitely. People will gladly tell you how crazy you are to go after anything "unknown" because you will have to give up your "known," your given life. How dare you do that, right? Who are you to think that you can do better, feel better and live better, right? It was already too hard to get here. And if you pay attention, these people sound just like that defense team in your head. ⭐ I wonder why, though. ⭐ Could it be because those are the thoughts and the opinions of others, repeatedly uploaded to your Shiny little head time and time again so you would subconsciously produce these counter arguments against your deepest, ultimate desires? No wonder you get stuck within your head, my dear.

I remember my own experience of the "transit life," my Shiny. Oh, yes, it felt very weird going against the force of the crowd and leaving behind everything I had built. But the most interesting part was the reaction I had received from many people in my environment. Raised eyebrows, suspicious looks, surprised faces and dropping jaws, "oh, my gosh" feedbacks and screaming feedbacks. They were all shocked, my dear. They were all in a very interesting and a highly "criticizing" shock mode, if I may. ⭐ At the same time, I felt incredible! I had never felt more certain in my entire being! The most popular question I received was: *"Are you crazy? You have a great job and an executive position. How can you leave your career just like that after 10 years? You don't even know what you are going to do in United States!"* And my most popular answer was, *"Well, I know I have a great job and a great future career ahead of me in my company, but if I have been able to achieve all these things, then I can achieve more!"* By the way, I really enjoyed my job and truly put my heart in it and achieved great results. I loved my boss and the management team, I loved the international travel and the power I had, as the head of marketing, but I loved the "cosmic calling" inside of me more!

And that's how my journey of transformation as a galactic being started, in the moment of my big, heartfelt, committed decision.

YOU ARE A STAR!
GO GALACTIC

GALACTIC BEINGS – in need of ELECTRIFIED COSMIC ENERGY!

They are the ones who can cosmically design their own shining path of success, fulfillment and happiness and joy. They are the ones who can go against the wind when there is a bigger purpose to achieve. They are the ones who can stand naked in the crowd as who they are with their full identity, with their deep, juicy, even-energy core, because they are on a divine mission to lead the galaxies, the worlds, the systems, the people and all the beings inside the systems to a better place called being "LIVE" and feeling "alive." **Galactic leaders** are the ones who can ask, *"Am I living my truth with the best of who I can be and actualizing my cosmic potential? Am I living an inspired shining galactic life and also inspiring others to become a better version of themselves?* They live in a divine place called the "**cosmic life**." Therefore, they are working toward helping others to question their given and transit lives. ☆

The boredom, meaninglessness, aimlessness or being just "OK" are not really the emotional repertoire of a galactic being because of the joy and the purpose these cosmic beings feel in engaging in new and challenging activities. While the physical beings or the transit beings see life as mysterious, unknown or unpredictable, a galactic leader finds life very magical, wondrous and cosmically meaningful. We galactic leaders, my friend, don't feel disengaged or restless because of the trappings of our lives. We are not going to accept any given life without a question. We are not going to take any statement without busting the obvious assumptions that even the one who makes it is not aware of. That is because we don't take life lightly, we take life seriously and deliciously with Swedish chocolate and lavender martini on the side. ☆ We get what an experience is; we experience what we get with our full presence and our conscious decisions complementing the complete joyfulness.

To the physical and the transit beings, reaching at a galactic level seems like an unattainable star in the sky, since we galactic beings are fully charged, focused, energetic, loving and look like one without any problems. ⭐ But one thing they need to understand is that the secret is not having any problems, which is humanly, cosmically and galactically not possible; the secret is having the skills to handle with or to minimize the problems! The secret is our recovery rate! It's our ability to elegantly recover from the unpleasant happenings. That's all! ⭐ Galactic beings are also human beings my dear, you remember that, right? ⭐ Just checking ⭐ So, they also have the same operational and executional systems like anyone else, with one big, enormous difference: They make their own systems work for them, instead of those systems' making them work. ⭐ They simply apply all the galactic, cosmic and universal laws that are available out there to their days, to their lives and to their minds! And boom! MAGIC! And boom! GALACTIC! And boom! STARDOM SMILE & SHINE! ⭐

That's what happened to me! After having gone through so many limited, physical but not spiritual life experiences, trying to reframe life's happenings and getting really good at them, I knew I had to change something. I was completely logical, repeating Einstein's definition of insanity to myself, looking for solutions: Doing the same thing over and over again and expecting different results. Galactic Rules of Applied Wisdom #9, Shiny. ⭐ If it ain't working, it's changing, my dear! ⭐

And finally, in my search for soul, I felt God's hands on my shoulders, calling me for a different work. My Shiny god was telling me to do something completely different and she was promising that I could get closer to her, if I chose that. I could definitely get closer to her by feeling happier, fuller, shinier and definitely more alive as me! That's what being spiritual was to me—feeling that I am right next to my Shiny god in whatever I do, whenever it is, wherever I do and however I do it. ⭐ That kind of a feeling would be my ultimate feeling!!! The very first of Cosmic Law of the Universe: The Law of Divine Oneness! THE ULTIMATE PURPOSE!

So when I heard my god whisper into my ears, I knew it was she calling. But the choice was still mine. I knew it. But I also knew that it was NOW or NEVER *(like the Now or Never song)!*

So I applied the Cosmic Laws of the Universe #8: The Law of Action. I Be-Live'd in my power and my ability to Be-Live in me and I took action and moved back to Los Angeles! Oh, gosh. The best days of my life. Chasing a dream, full of life and energy. Simply on fire *(like Alicia Keys' Girl on Fire song)*! To get my life back! To live again, to breathe again! To be me again! ⭐ I did it! Right away!

And when I was doing that, I made sure that I focused only and merely on my reason why, which was the conversation I had with my Shiny god. ⭐ Simply my feelings, my strong, unstoppable and clear feelings deep inside. More real than anything else in life! And I also had to protect my confidence, forget about my weaknesses, forget about the worries and the fear of the unknown and also watch out for bad advice, Shiny. ⭐ Oh, yes. That is so importantly, my sparkly head. Remember Galactic Rule # 7, dear? Who you surround yourself with is who you eventually become! So I really had to watch out for the bad advice coming from the people that I didn't want to become, advice about what I should do, how I should do it, etc. As if they have done a better job! I knew that I did not have all the resources like people and money, but I knew that I was resourceful (Galactic Rules of Applied Wisdom # 8)!

And I knew that I was becoming a galactic leader of my life!!! I WAS ELECTRIFIED! It felt so incredible! I needed ELECTRIFIED COSMIC ENERGY to lead my galactic path, Shiny and happy. ⭐ So I generated electrified cosmic energy. I needed strong beliefs to move on and I generated strong beliefs. I needed money to invest in myself and I found my way to make money. I needed to have more time to invest in my growth so I turned off the TV, I shut down unnecessary sources of information in my life, I kept focusing and refocusing and so I generated more time. I needed to get better in the English language so I read more, spoke more and practiced more, and I generated better English. I needed to know what to do so I searched for many many different ways and I chose the best among them and generated my knowing. I needed to know how to do it and I studied more to learn and I also generated my know-how. I needed experience and I did it over and over again, and I also generated my experience. I needed to stay positive in times of troubles so I filled my mind with positive thoughts, movies, songs and feelings, so I also generated my positivity. I needed to know the right kind of people and so I went ahead and I met the right kind of people.

I did whatever it took, Shiny. I was committed. I was on a mission. I was on a cosmic mission.

So I followed and applied all those cosmic and galactic laws of the universe along my way and, yes, my Shiny, they worked! Here I am, born again from the ashes of my physical and transit beings, as a new Shiny galactic leader, to be a part of our cosmic and galactic federation!

So you can do it, too!

WE ARE NOT ONLY HERE TO BE OURSELVES BUT ALSO TO LIVE OURSELVES.

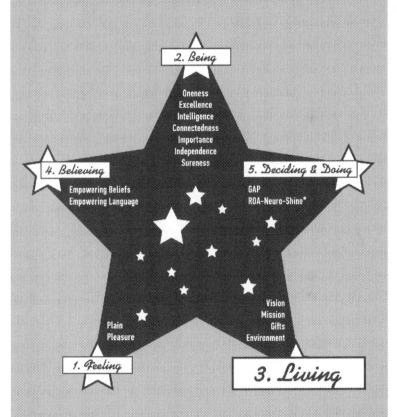

3. LIVING

Well, well, well, my dear galactic friend, Shiny. By now, you should know that every change has multiple layers and that every being has multiple existential needs to fulfill so as to become that glorious superstar to shine bright in her galactic path. And so far, we have gone through the first two steps of feeling and being before we do any sort of deciding. And now it's about time that we talk about how you'll be living.

This part is all about your existential reasoning and the meaning of your galactic being. Most of human beings, especially the ones with lower consciousness, will never get to this level of advanced cosmic understanding, my darling. And that's what makes this part exceptionally important and significant, because this is the part that you claim your right to be whoever you truly want to be or, better said, whoever you were meant to be.

If you remind your beautiful self that you are originally made of stardust and therefore you are a Shiny happy galactic superstar just like the ones you stare at night, it will be so easy for you to think about the reason of your existence. Isn't that right, my dear? So, that's what I am talking about. ⭐

These are the four pillars of your life that we will be covering in order to clarify the way you want to be living, darling:

1) **Environment**
2) **Gifts**
3) **Mission**
4) **Vision**

ENVIRONMENT	★ Relationships ★ Language
GIFTS	★ Natural talents ★ Learned skills
MISSION	★ Values ★ Beliefs
PURPOSE/VISION	★ Identity ★ Universal contribution

1) ENVIRONMENT:

A galactic leader can only shine as bright as the light she receives from the other galactic sources around her.

So let's start with measuring your current behaviors, relationships and your everyday language to see where you are with your environment, darling. Go ahead and give your honest answers to the following questions by just selecting one of the multiple choices:

1) I make my point easily and effectively and I get what I want every time I interact with my **immediate family members**.

Not at all   Not likely   Likely   Very likely   All the time

2) I make my point easily and effectively and I get what I want every time I interact with my **extended family members**.

Not at all   Not likely   Likely   Very likely   All the time

3) I make my point easily and effectively and I get what I want every time I interact with my **friends.**

Not at all   Not likely   Likely   Very likely   All the time

4) I make my point easily and effectively and I get what I want every time I interact with <u>the people I **hire** to work with.</u>

Not at all   Not likely   Likely   Very likely   All the time

5) I make my point easily and effectively and I get what I want every time I interact with <u>the **people that hire me** to work with them.</u>

Not at all   Not likely   Likely   Very likely   All the time

6) I make my point easily and effectively and I get what I want every time I interact with <u>the **new people** I meet.</u>

Not at all   Not likely   Likely   Very likely   All the time

Based upon your answers, do you see any pattern in your relationships? For example, you might be getting along very well and getting all the results you want with the people that hire you and the people you just meet, along with your friends, yet you might feel like you are not even able to communicate well with your family members and the people you hire, or any other combination. Sound familiar?

In this case, my glitter, it's your time to pay close attention to the WHO aspect of your environment. Sometimes it is unfortunately the people around us who block us from LIVING a life in our own terms. And as weird as it sounds, sometimes it is the very YOU that blocks you from having a blast with the people around you, my dear!

How will you know if it is not you but the people around you that limit your LIVING? Well, honey, you will definitely know this one easily. In life, it is your relationships with the people around you that creates the most meaning for you, sparkly heads. After all, aren't we all here to shine as bright as we can? A galactic leader can only shine as bright as the light she receives from the other sources around her. For this reason, you are required to be selective of your own environment, my superstar.

YOU ARE A STAR!
BE SELECTIVE
OF YOUR OWN
GALAXY

It's just a matter of combining some galactic and universal laws together to figure this out. Remember the cosmic law of divine oneness and the law of correspondence, which means that you are stardust and your physical reality represents only the 10 percent of your overall reality? Do you also remember the universal principle of the power of knowledge, meaning that if you don't have the knowledge level of the other people around you, you cannot possibly give that knowledge to somebody else? Well, Shiny, you will come to see that they cannot give that glamorous shining light to you because they do not have it, my dear!

They cannot represent your reality because you are the only who creates your own reality. But they are obviously in your life for a reason. Negative people with unhappy faces and complaining attitudes, somewhat disapproving, somewhat criticizing you or others in life; with their know-it-all preaching, again and again resenting, low-self-esteem functioning, jealousy and everyday victim mentality are very easy to catch in your environment. Am I right? You know some people in life are committed to disagree with you and dis-ease your day, that even if you were nominated for a Nobel Prize in your kindness or what not, they will do whatever it takes to make you feel something is wrong with you? Well, these are the ones I am talking about my, Shiny head. As ironic as it may sound, sweetheart, they may have the best intentions, and yet they may do the most damage by just not being or living on the same level as you, creating more drama and chaos, and focusing on the problems in your life. Sound familiar? Well your job is to realize <u>WHO</u> these people are in your environment and simply ask this question to your Shiny self: "What am I learning from this person or from this experience with this person to grow and create a higher version of myself?" Because, honey, as you will also come to realize that nothing in this life will never ever leave you without teaching you something you need to learn. So once again, what are you learning from these people? When you get your answer, take it in, accept it and apply it in your future relationships. And as for these types of people in your environment, my darling, I'd say, simply RUN AWAY from this kind of pain and let them go through their own journey in their own map of realities to be transformed, somewhere far far away from you.

How will you know if it is <u>you</u>, blocking the GALACTIC version of U? Well, I know that it requires a great deal of self-awareness and some basic understanding and measurement of your current relationships. You can simply examine your answers to the above questions and if you happen to find yourself having difficulty in interacting with most of the people around you, then it might be an obvious sign. Or you might as well be honest with yourself to admit if you fall into any of the categories that I mentioned above when I was giving the example of "negative people" that are blocking your superstar version. Because you will feel deep down if you are not giving your 100 percent to the people around you or you if you are not giving your 100 percent to yourself. After all this clarity, you will definitely know if it is a part of you that's blocking you.

YOU ARE A STAR!
AVOID NEGATIVE PEOPLE

Your **language** will also manifest WHO is blocking YOU from LIVING a GALACTIC VERSION OF YOU, my Shiny head. The words you use in your everyday life and the affirmations you choose to adapt in your overall journey will simply manifest where you stand in your life.

The quality of your communication with yourself = the quality of your communication with others.

The quality of your language = the quality of your life.

What are some words that you tell to yourself on a day-to-day basis? Let's excerpt them out of your mind and put it right in front of your eyes for your awareness, my darling:

I am …
… …

I am ... ...
... ...

I am ... ...
... ...

I am not... ... ...
... ...

I am not... ... ...
... ...

I am not... ... ...
... ...

I do ... ...
... ...

I do ... ...
... ...

I do ... ...
... ...

I do not ... ...
... ...

I do not ... ...
... ...

I do not ... ...
... ...

I can ... ...
... ...

I can … … … … … … … … … … … … … … … … … …
… … … … … … … … … … … … … … … … … … … …

I can … … … … … … … … … … … … … … … … … …
… … … … … … … … … … … … … … … … … … … …

I cannot… … … … … … … … … … … … … … … … …
… … … … … … … … … … … … … … … … … … … …

I cannot… … … … … … … … … … … … … … … … …
… … … … … … … … … … … … … … … … … … … …

I cannot… … … … … … … … … … … … … … … … …
… … … … … … … … … … … … … … … … … … … …

I have   … … … … … … … … … … … … … … … … …
… … … … … … … … … … … … … … … … … … … …

I have   … … … … … … … … … … … … … … … … …
… … … … … … … … … … … … … … … … … … … …

I have   … … … … … … … … … … … … … … … … …
… … … … … … … … … … … … … … … … … … … …

I have not … … … … … … … … … … … … … … … …
… … … … … … … … … … … … … … … … … … … …

I have not … … … … … … … … … … … … … … … …
… … … … … … … … … … … … … … … … … … … …

I have not … … … … … … … … … … … … … … … …
… … … … … … … … … … … … … … … … … … … …

You see the results for yourself and you decide how QUALITY your own language is. And right after that, please also use the below sheet to generate some fresh language for yourself, for your relationships with others and also for your quality markers:

CREATION (Self)	EXPRESSION (Others)	CELEBRATION (Shiny & Happy Life)
I am choosing these 3 words as my highest personal values to create myself, my invisible forces inside	I am choosing these 3 words as my highest social values to express myself when I am with others	I am choosing these 3 words as my highest spiritual values to celebrate my life regardless of what happens
My reason for choosing my first word is...	My reason for choosing my first word is...	My reason for choosing my first word is...
My reason for choosing my second word is...	My reason for choosing my second word is...	My reason for choosing my second word is...
My reason for choosing my third word is...	My reason for choosing my third word is...	My reason for choosing my third word is...

At this point, your job is to repeat them each and every day consistently and enthusiastically. Remember the levels of learning, Shiny? So you know that you can regenerate a whole new vocabulary for yourself with just repeating them enough times. It is the power of your mind and the power of your re-framing technology of NLP, my dear. Use it in your everyday life and get the most amazing results for yourself. Start practicing now and we'll come back to the idea of LANGUAGE later in the next chapter, as well.

That's how important it is. For every galactic leader, there needs to be a galactic language that wows the world! ⭐

YOU ARE A STAR!
USE WOW WORDS

2) GIFTS:

Your gifts are your unique talents that you are born with, or simply master throughout your cosmic experience, my dear starshine. According to neuroscientists, there are several categories of giftedness, as in multiple intelligences, and they are in linguistic, logico-mathematical, musical, spatial, kinesthetic, interpersonal, intrapersonal, naturalistic and existential areas. And within these areas lies other distinctive gifts one can have from birth or build by experience, such as charisma, persuasion, presence, leadership skills like risk taking, public speaking, strategic thinking, synergy focus, results-oriented goal setting, critical mind mapping, rapport building, emotional intelligence skills like self-awareness, self-regulation, motivation, empathy, social skills and other giftedness qualities such as analytical intelligence, creative intelligence, practical intelligence, etc.

Do you know what your cosmic talents are? Go get your Shiny pen and start listing a minimum of 21 cosmic gifts that you have in your galactic existence:

1._____
2._____
3._____
4._____
5._____
6._____
7._____
8._____
9._____
10._____
11._____
12._____
13._____
14._____
15._____
16._____
17._____
18._____
19._____
20._____
21._____

You know, sparky head, 21 is a cosmic number. That's why we are listing 21 gifts of yours and repeating your galactic language 21 days in a row. You kinda know what to do now, darling. You will go ahead and repeat these 21 gifts of yours 21 days in a row, in that loud, firm and sharp voice of yours. It takes 21 days to fire up the two neighboring neurons together in your brain, so that they end up wiring up together, remember? ☆

3 & 4) MISSION & VISION:

And let's continue with what makes you alive in your being, your personal galactic **mission & vision** statement, darling. In order for you to have the best life ever lived, you must have a clear reason WHY you are here to begin with. And I know that this is a deep issue and a deep, multi-dimensional subject that you might never have thought about. That's why you are going to enjoy writing your personal, galactic mission & vision statement, my darling. Here are some questions for you to consider as a guideline into writing your own Shiny galactic mission & vision statement. Just answer them by staying connected to your soul and you will gradually build a sense of meaning in your mind:

YOUR COSMIC VALUES:

These are the most important things for me in life:... ...

... ...

... ...

... ...

... ...

... ...

YOUR UNIVERSAL BELIEFS:

These are my fundamental beliefs that empower me every time I think about them: ... ...

... ...

... ...

... ...

... ...

... ...

YOUR GALACTIC PERFORMANCE:

I am at my best performance when … … … … … … …
… … … … … … … … … … … … … … … … … … … …
… … … … … … … … … … … … … … … … … … … …
… … … … … … … … … … … … … … … … … … … …
… … … … … … … … … … … … … … … … … … … …
… … … … … … … … … … … … … … … … … … … …

I am at my worst performance when … … … … … … …
… … … … … … … … … … … … … … … … … … … …
… … … … … … … … … … … … … … … … … … … …
… … … … … … … … … … … … … … … … … … … …
… … … … … … … … … … … … … … … … … … … …
… … … … … … … … … … … … … … … … … … … …

YOUR COSMIC PASSION:

What do I really love to do professionally? … … … … …
… … … … … … … … … … … … … … … … … … … …
… … … … … … … … … … … … … … … … … … … …
… … … … … … … … … … … … … … … … … … … …
… … … … … … … … … … … … … … … … … … … …
… … … … … … … … … … … … … … … … … … … …

What do I really love to do in my personal life? … … …
… … … … … … … … … … … … … … … … … … … …
… … … … … … … … … … … … … … … … … … … …
… … … … … … … … … … … … … … … … … … … …
… … … … … … … … … … … … … … … … … … … …
… … … … … … … … … … … … … … … … … … … …

SUPERSTAR TALENTS:

My natural talents and gifts are: (*examples may be art, music, decision making, being a friend, etc.*) ... ...
... ...
... ...
... ...
... ...
... ...

IMAGINATION:

If I had unlimited time and resources, and knew I could not fail, what would I choose to do? ... ...
... ...
... ...
... ...
... ...
... ...

VISUALIZATION:

Imagine your life as an epic journey with you as the hero/heroine of the story. What do you imagine your journey to be about? Complete the following statement by describing what you are doing, who is it for, why you are doing it, and what the journey's results are.

My life's journey is ... ...
... ...
... ...
... ...
... ...
... ...

IDENTITY:

Imagine your 80th birthday now. Who will be there with you? Can you imagine? What identity statement would you like them to make about your life?   … … … … … … …
… … … … … … … … … … … … … … … … … … … …
… … … … … … … … … … … … … … … … … … … …
… … … … … … … … … … … … … … … … … … … …
… … … … … … … … … … … … … … … … … … … …
… … … … … … … … … … … … … … … … … … … …

CONTRIBUTION

What do I consider to be my most important future contribution to the most important people in my life? …
… … … … … … … … … … … … … … … … … … … …
… … … … … … … … … … … … … … … … … … … …
… … … … … … … … … … … … … … … … … … … …
… … … … … … … … … … … … … … … … … … … …
… … … … … … … … … … … … … … … … … … … …

INTEGRITY

Are there things I feel I really should do or change, even though I may have dismissed such thoughts many times? What are they?

… … … … … … … … … … … … … … … … … … … …
… … … … … … … … … … … … … … … … … … … …
… … … … … … … … … … … … … … … … … … … …
… … … … … … … … … … … … … … … … … … … …
… … … … … … … … … … … … … … … … … … … …
… … … … … … … … … … … … … … … … … … … …

INFLUENCE

Imagine you could invite to dinner three people who have influenced you the most—past or present. Write their names in the boxes below. Then record the one quality or attribute you admire most in these people.

... ...

... ...

... ...

... ...

... ...

... ...

PERSON 1 NAME:... ... ...

QUALITY:... ... ...

PERSON 2 NAME:... ... ...

QUALITY:... ... ...

PERSON 3 NAME:... ... ...

QUALITY:... ... ...

BALANCE

Let's think of balance as a state of fulfillment and renewal in each of the four dimensions: physical, mental, social/emotional and spiritual. What are the single most important things you can do in each of these areas that will have the greatest positive impact on your life and help you achieve a sense of balance?

Physical

....
....
....
....
....
....

Mental

....
....
....
....
....

Social/Emotional

....
....
....
....
....

Spiritual

....
....
....
....
....

YOUR GALACTIC MISSION:

This is my cosmic mission that I am choosing for my life with the light of all that I am and all that I have: ... ...

... ...

... ...

... ...

... ...

YOUR GALACTIC VISION:

This is my cosmic vision that I am choosing for my cosmic orbit: ... ...

... ...

... ...

... ...

For now, you can congratulate yourself on a job well done, Shiny! You now can tell your friends about your newly stated purpose in life! What makes you **Be-Live in U!**

Also remember, Shiny, life is an ongoing process and so is your mission statement.

Over the years, as your circumstances change your priorities will also change. Your goals and dreams will change. That's totally OK and also expected, darling, because change means growth. As you grow, transform and broaden your horizons, allow yourself the freedom to expand and refine your mission & vision statement.

The next step is learning **how to live** your mission. Maybe it's easy, but maybe it takes some guidance. And I am here to help. Learn more about my NLP training on How to Be, How to Live and How to Be-Live in U as a Galactic Leader here.

Life is a journey. And your mission statement is your map honey. Go have fun with your galactic friends and create the most unforgettable game you can ever play! ⭐

WE ARE HERE TO BELIEVE SO THAT WE CAN ACHIEVE!

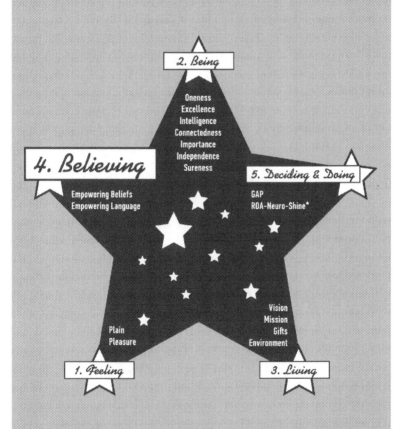

4. BELIEVING

In order to win anything in life, first you have to believe in it. If success were a being, its heart would absolutely beat at believing.

I want you to notice something, Shiny. All the universal laws, the rules and the principles I shared above were all, in a way, thought filters for you, right? What is a thought filter? Let's chunk that down! If there is a thought and if there is a filter, you only filter your thoughts through what you Be-Live and what you don't Be-Live as your filters. When you Be-Live in some thoughts or ethics and morality strongly as convictions, they become thicker filters as values in your mind. And the thicker your filters are the thicker your neuro muscles are. Firmly shaping the way you look at life, situations and people in it, since your neuro-muscles are not letting any stranger thoughts or different ideas in. In the end, in what you Be-Live is the way you live.

Then, you must really dig into the realm of your beliefs and find out what you Be-Live and what you don't Be-Live. I mean, if you want to make lemonade but if you don't Be-Live in the taste of your lemons, you can't make lemonade! C'mon! You have to have some kind of belief to carry on, but not these disempowering ones to stop you from what you want to be-do or have, darling.

Within the dark, juicy and fast-paced kingdom of your beliefs upstairs in your mind, these are the steps that we are going to hack into together:

* **Be aware of your Disempowering Beliefs – *Neurological***

* **Activate your Empowering Beliefs – *Neuro-logical***

* **Be aware of your Disempowering Language – *Linguistic***

* **Activate your Empowering Language – *Linguistic***

EMPOWERING BELIEFS

Be aware of your **Disempowering Beliefs** – *Neurological*

So let's start with your disempowering beliefs first. Get your pen and paper that you always use for these exercise and start listing what you don't Be-Live in:

1. I don't Be-Live in... ... ...
... ...

2. I don't Be-Live in... ... ...
... ...

3. I don't Be-Live that I can ... ...
... ...

4. I don't Be-Live that I can ... ...
... ...

5. I don't Be-Live that I am ... ...
... ...

6. I don't Be-Live that I am ... ...
... ...

7. I don't Be-Live that life is ... ...
... ...

8. I don't Be-Live that life can be … … … … … … … …
… …

9. I don't Be-Live that people are … … … … … … … …
… …

10. I don't Be-Live that people can be   … … … … … …
… …

Well, obviously whatever you listed or wanted to list more, are your disempowering beliefs in your Shiny mind as BIG, FAT filters, stopping you to take action! But, they are all in your head, hello? I don't see them and I don't have them, so they don't really exist! They are some illusions in your head! Remember FEARS? Yes, that's what they are. And ironically, you everything you are running away from is your head, darling. You can't run away from your beautiful head, can you?

So stop it! And face it! There is no such thing that you don't Be-Live you are capable or you don't Be-Live you are smart enough or you are worthy enough or good enough to be successful and get rich! Yes you can do it and yes you do Be-Live in it and yes you will! If anybody else can do it, you also can do it! Just step up to become a better version of yourself and show the world who you can really be!!!

Activate your **Empowering Beliefs – *Neurological***

So, let's re-do this exercise and let's reframe everything you said to your Shiny galactic self, my darling! I want you to write down every single sentence from the scratch and reframe each and every one of them in a believingly positive language that can motivate you and activate your soul! Go!

233

1. I do Be-Live in   … … … … … … … … … … … …
… … … … … … … … … … … … … … … … … …

2. I do Be-Live in   … … … … … … … … … … … …
… … … … … … … … … … … … … … … … … …

3. I do Be-Live that I can … … … … … … … … … …
… … … … … … … … … … … … … … … … … …

4. I do Be-Live that I can … … … … … … … … … …
… … … … … … … … … … … … … … … … … …

5. I do Be-Live that I am … … … … … … … … … …
… … … … … … … … … … … … … … … … … …

6. I do Be-Live that I am … … … … … … … … … …
… … … … … … … … … … … … … … … … … …

7. I do Be-Live that life is … … … … … … … … … …
… … … … … … … … … … … … … … … … … …

8. I do Be-Live that life can be … … … … … … … … …
… … … … … … … … … … … … … … … … … …

9. I do Be-Live that people are … … … … … … … … …
… … … … … … … … … … … … … … … … … …

10. I do Be-Live that people can be   … … … … … …
… … … … … … … … … … … … … … … … … …

And now, I want you to read these 10 new positively rephrased galactic belief sentences three times with a firm, loud voice! Go!

Are you done? I Be-Live you are. I mean, you are not going to cheat the world of your own empowering beliefs, are you? ⭐ I know you won't. So please, if you haven't repeated these 10 sentences three times with your firm, confidant loud and certain voice, do it now!

OK, now you know what it is and how it feels. As awesome as it feels, this is what you will be doing 21 days in a row before you go to bed or the first thing you wake up in the morning. Deal? This is your magic recipe to have a shinier and happier belief system my dear. I know you get me. ⭐

Listen, darling, there is no right or wrong in this path of life. I really want you to get it. Any right or wrong combination you might have in your Shiny little head will totally belong to you and shape you for whoever you want to become! So all these things that you are doing right now in my exclusive workshop for you in this book, is not for the purpose of finding your "self" baby, it is all for the purpose of creating your "self" as a gorgeous glamorous galactic star! Get it? Your galactic path is not meant to be found, it is meant to be created by you! As the galactic leader in U!

We are all here, trying to be, not trying to do or to have things, honey. We think we are here to have more money, bigger houses and better cars and yes we all want all these, not because owning them will make us become happier, but because we become somebody who has the power to buy them, who can afford them and who can enjoy more happiness and more pleasure with them!

EMPOWERING LANGUAGE

Be aware of your **Disempowering Language** – *Linguistic*

Well, now that you are pretty much aware of your empowering and disempowering beliefs and how to easily re-frame a disempowering belief as an empowering one, you are neurologically equipped to BELIEVE in whatever you want to believe, darling. Congratulations! ☆

It is now time to analyze your everyday language, my dear, because not only the problems you have sometimes is the way you use language, but you also do have a greater chance to set yourself up higher in lifebecause you know HOW to use your linguistic skills. Does that ring a bell?

Think about all the cool people you met in your life. And think about how they made you feel. You either felt *inspiration* or *desperation* when you were with them, depending on what kind of comparison process you went through in your Shiny little head. Remember, it is not WHAT process you choose to do in your neurological process, it is HOW you actually do that process.

For example, if you met a very successful person who has already achieved the results that you have been dreaming about for years, you can choose to feel the "*inspiration*" just by recognizing how far she has come to where she is today and what you can learn from her to get closer to your own results. Or you might as well choose to feel the "*desperation*" just by recognizing how unsuccessful you are when you compare yourself with her. It is just a matter of neurological perspective toward the new information you are receiving (her success story in this case) and a following choice you make, as simple as that!

In order for you to be able to recognize her "inspiration" you have a great mind work to do: To shut down your own emotional signals and focus only on her story, not yours!⭐ It is all about her now, where she started, how she started, how she moved forward, what struggles she went through, what she learned from her journey, how she feels now, etc. And you are fortunately listening to someone who can really spark a fire in you to activate your own personal power to achieve what you have been wanting to achieve. You just need to accept that it's only about her, and there is no need to bring up your story and compare it with hers. First of all you have all the contextual framework differences like personal experiences, expertise, motivations, personalities, support systems and proximity factors to the resources you need to get the same results, so if you do compare yourself with her, it would be like, Why is this apple greener than the color of the orange. ⭐ Get it? So my lovely, just believe in "inspiration" and learn from other experiences in life!

YOU ARE A STAR!
FIND INSPIRATION

And once again, you can only do this through separating yourself from your emotional signals. Those signals might show up as negative voices associated with your disempowering beliefs, or your unsatisfied need to feel better, to feel more significant or superior. That might also show up as negative voices translated into your negative linguistic skills. If you ever let those negative voices show up in your language with others, you simply are in *"desperation,"* my star to be, not in *"inspiration"* at all. You simply accept and implement that there is only your story in this cosmic universe and that's it. There are no other journeys to wonder about, and there are no other beings to get curious about because there is only you! ⭐ Sounds a little funny, doesn't it? ⭐ Well, if you are 16 or 18, you might as well exactly like this, and that's perfectly fine! There is an aging and maturing factor, after all. Yet, the sooner you realize what your galactic journey is about the better my dear, especially of you are on a galactic leader path! And don't you really wanna learn how other galactic friends are operating in their own paths, especially if they are shining a little brighter than you? You sure want to learn HOW to shine bright like a diamond right my Shiny? That's what I am talking about, my dear!

So then, let's move on with one of their secrets to shine a little brighter: Their language! And let's take a look at what is your everyday linguistic magic is. Are you ready?

Get your Shiny pen and start writing down 10 sentences that you use on a daily basis, either by yourself or with others that are really not so positive and simply full of disempowering language:

1. …

2. …

3. …

4. …

5. …

6. …

7. …

8. …

9. …

10. … … … … … … … … … … … … … … … … … … …

Please be brutally honest when getting your disempowering language off your chest my darling. This is your step to be aware of it and it is really crucial. If you don't know what to fix, chances are you might always be broken!!! Oh, my! Can you imagine? What a dark place to be in! Run from it!

Remember the formula for change?

CHANGE = AWARENESS + WILLINGNESS

Well, now that you have become aware of your limiting linguistic patterns, then you are only your "willingness" away from changing your language from disempowering to outstandingly empowering! Just like re-framing your beliefs, we are going to go ahead and re-frame your language as well, my star shine!

Activate your **Empowering Language** – *Linguistic*

Let's willingly, consciously re-frame your linguistic patterns in such a way as to put you in your heightened moods and activate a better version of yourself, my darling. Choose some really EMPOWERING, ENERGIZING and EXCITING language below to write down your new empowering sentences to replace with your disempowering sentences:

Some empowering words to be inspired by:

Inspiration Power Mission Change Energy Exciting Happy Transformational Empowering Committed Attached Associated Leader I AM Freedom LOVE Brave Bold Encouraging Being present Intelligent Caring Discipline Empathy Confident Skills Strength Faith Wisdom Contribution Understanding Accepting

1. ... ...

2. ... ...

3. ... ...

4. ... ...

5. ... ...

6. ... ...

7. ... ...

8. ... ...

9. ... ...

10. ... ...

And now, like you did before with your empowering beliefs, I want you to read these 10 new positively rephrased and empowering galactic sentences three times with a firm, loud voice! Go!

Are you done? Again, you are not going to cheat the world of your own empowering language, are you? ☆ I know you won't. So please, if you haven't repeated these 10 sentences three times with your firm, confident loud and certain voice, do it now!

OK, now you know what it is and how it feels again. As awesome as it feels, this is what you will be doing 21 days in a row before you go to bed or the first thing you wake up in the morning. Deal? If you want, go ahead and take a picture of these pages and place them somewhere you can see clearly every single day, preferably next to your bed.

These empowering beliefs and empowering sentences are your magic recipe to have a shinier and happier belief system, my dear. You are ready to BELIEVE. Congratulations! Use them every day, BELIEVE in your own galactic power and be empowered!

Should you need my help in getting your beliefs transformed, you know where to find me!  www.Be-LiveinU.com

YOU ARE A STAR!
BE EMPOWERED

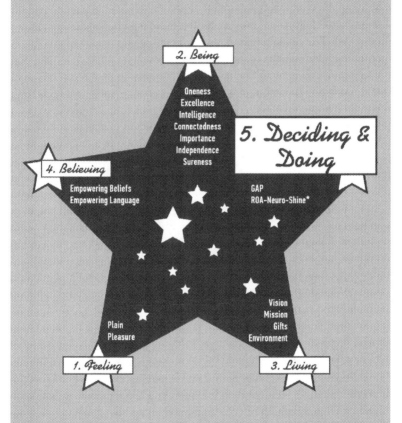

5. DECIDING & DOING

Galactic leaders are extremely good at making right and bright decisions, my dear Shiny. Wondering why? Not only because they are very much aware of their true, shining power within, but also they know what to do with it. ⭐ You know what we say, Shiny: *"Repetition is the **queen** of your skills."* Wanna know why? Just check out your bicep muscles for me, would you? Now, feel the strength of your arm and tell me how skillful your biceps are. That's why, my Shiny. ⭐ And galactic leaders happen to have plenty of these skillful muscles in their beautiful heads. Because they know that their ultimate return from repeating an action will be nothing but their own satisfaction.

So you need to foresee what your return, your result, is going to be from your decisions and your actions, my lovely. I want you to understand, Shiny, that a decision is a serious brain activity. By making a decision you are literally drawing your own road to follow. You are designing your own galactic path. You are choosing your next big thing in life. You are programming your own mind to wire in that way instead of another way. You are re-designing your brain and re-creating yourself. That's why a decision is a serious business of your mind, my sparky head. And that's also why we covered all those cosmic and galactic laws of the universe, all those fantastic rules of application with all those exercises in the previous chapters before you come to a point of decision. Because it is in your big, heartfelt decisions that you shape your galactic path! And it is in your Shiny neurons that you make your everyday Shiny decisions, my darling!

Did you already feel the need for you to have Shiny neurons in your head? ⭐ Great! ⭐ We'll talk about that very entertaining method of Neuro-Shine in a moment, but first, let's get you a plan!

Well, as we all know, it is very easy for everyone to talk the talk, but is it really that easy to walk the walk? You need to know that there is nothing better than an <u>action</u> for a human being to feel alive, my dear Shiny! Especially, galactic leaders need meaningful, galactic actions to shine in their cosmic lives! Or maybe I should only say, *"Actions speak louder than words,"* and *"No action creates no hurts"*:

> ➤ **GAP: Create a Galactic Action Plan**

For every decision, you need an action. And for every action, you need a plan and you need preparation. It is about time that we put together a nice Shiny galactic action plan for you, my dear.

And for that galactic plan, you need a galactic purpose, right, my darling? So, just like we started analyzing where you were in life with a list of questions at the beginning of this book of shine, now we are going to finalize your plan to shine by finding where your heart is, my dear Shiny. Go grab your sparkling pen and just let your heart move your fingers, my galactic friend.

CHOOSING YOUR GALACTIC PURPOSE

1. What are your personal interests?

… …
… …
… …
… …

2. What do you love to do? What brings you JOY?

... ...
... ...
... ...
... ...

3. What three non-fiction books would you have liked to have written about?

... ...
... ...
... ...
... ...

4. What would you do for free?

... ...
... ...
... ...
... ...

5. What would others ask you for your advice and perspective?

... ...
... ...
... ...
... ...

6. What challenges have you overcome in your life?

... ...
... ...
... ...
... ...

7. What are your god-given, inherent and natural talents?

… …
… …
… …
… …

8. What are your best characteristics and strengths you
   enjoy?

… …
… …
… …
… …

9. How can you help and serve others?

… …
… …
… …
… …

10.What was your biggest dream as a little girl? ⭐

… …
… …
… …
… …

11. Who do you want to serve?

… …
… …
… …
… …

12. At the end of your life, what would you have liked to be proud about yourself?

… …
… …
… …
… …

13. What do **U Be-Live** in the most?

… …
… …
… …
… …

14. How would you like to design your days?

… …
… …
… …
… …

15. List three ways to serve your society by combining all the information you have above:

… …
… …
… …
… …

And now, Shiny, choose the one that excites you the most, the one that makes you BE U with all that you have, LIVE U with everything you are, and makes U Be "**Live**" in U with every single cell inside of U my incredible galactic leader! Choose the one that makes you feel your life matters, your actions are needed and you have a galactic purpose to accomplish in this planet.

Choose the one that will create the BEST version of U! Choose the one that connects you to your soul, and to the universe inside of U. The one promises you the "Oneness" in everything you do and everything you are. Because you know, darling, it's your time to **SHINE!!!** ⭐

Now, let's talk about HOW you are going to design this galactic purpose as achievable items on your everyday to-do list. Because nothing Shiny comes that easy, sparkly. ⭐

It is in your ability to chunk down your ultimate destiny into little action steps that you may carry your shine to each and every day, my sweetie. So just commit to your ultimate goal and create small actions that you can take everyday, starting from NOW! If you can only increase your performance 1 percent everyday, you will outperform your normal self in as little as six months!

Linguistically a GAP is your distance from where you are today and where you ideally want to be. But in our galactic language, a GAP is your SMART map that includes the specific actions you need to take that will remove the distance between you and your ultimate goal. Simply, your GAP is your ultimate **Galactic Action Plan**. And your GAP will determine how bright you will be shining in your galactic system my, Shiny one. ⭐

In order to prepare your GAP, you will need to apply some strategies, such as KISS & SMART & SHINY.

KISS: Keep It Simple and Sexy.

Simple, because the simpler your language to your self the better the results your mind can create, my dear. It's just the software running on your head. ⭐

Sexy, because it will be easier to be committed to something you desire with every cell you have. ⭐

SMART: Specific, Measurable, Achievable, Realistic, Timely

Specific, so that you will know what exactly you are going after.

Measurable, so that you will be able to observe your progress and will know when exactly you get there.

Achievable, because every step counts in celebrating your success and even the simplest step you take toward your goal will make your brain release serotonin hormones for you to feel <u>happy about yourself and move forward to your goal with motivation.</u> ⭐

Realistic, not because you need to get real with where you are today, what your conditions are and what your resources are—not at all! On the contrary, I would encourage you to start visualizing as if you have already achieved your goal and walk backwards to your current conditions so that you can foresee all the resources you will need on your way back home. ⭐ In the end, we all know that a galactic leader will only shoot for a star! Not even clouds! Realistic because sometimes we really need to be aware of our natural talents, characteristics, learned skills vs. learnable skills so that we can also eliminate all the things we need to do but we really don't want to do, before we design our paths ahead.

Timely, because, my darling, your mind works best under pressure. And in here, time is your pressure. The deadline you set for yourself is the most precious motivational tool towards realizing any goal my dear. Think about your credit card payments and you will easily understand what I mean. ⭐

SHINY: Specific, Humanistic, Integrated, Natural, Yummy. ⭐

Specific pops up its head again! ⭐ In order for you to SHINE, my Shiny, you are already aware that you need to be crystal clear in HOW you are going to shine, right, my darling?

Humanistic, because you are an amazing, glittering galactic star and this is the most critical element that we forget in designing your galactic purpose, my dear. You are a treasure with what you know, what you do and who you are, because you are here to serve humanity anyway, my sparky.

Integrated, yes, of course, because everything you know will make the best sense when you are able to put them all together for your Shiny galactic purpose, dear. Think about it: If you know what you would do for free but you do not integrate this brilliant truth with your ultimate purpose, you might still be clueless about your path!!! Oh, no, that's not what you want, my diamond. You want knowledge and you want awareness, and you want them all integrated with your galactic purpose, my darling.

Natural, meaning it's already a part of you, that you would naturally do. Something that easily flows through you, so you would embrace it so effortlessly.

Yummy, because the more delicious your life is, the more connected, the more committed, and also the closer you are to it, my chocolate cake. ⭐ So make sure you design a good looking, happy sounding, great feeling, beautifully scented and mouth watering tasting action plan for you, my sparky head. ⭐ You've got all these senses—sparkle a piece of all into your galactic vision, darling!

Oh, by the way, remember the kinesiology technique I shared before? Oh, darling, please do use that technique to test your decision and do enjoy your body's confirmation on choosing your very own galactic purpose! ⭐

Here is HOW your **Galactic Action Plan** might look like, Shiny:

You know that it is in the moments of your big, clear, heartfelt and committed decisions that you shine your galactic path, darling! And for that decision to be made, you need your big, clear and heartfelt commitments, my star shine! That's why we went through all those chapters with you, weeding through the entire cluster in your head so that you could get clarity of your purpose. My purpose was helping you clarify your own purpose and make that big, heartfelt decision, my darling! Because with that decision you will create new behaviors and new rituals you enjoy. And with those new behaviors you will create new habits. And with those new habits you will create new beliefs. And with these new beliefs you will create your new identity! And with your new IDENTITY you will create your new DESTINY, my loveliest SHINY!

Your inner candle for a cosmic, galactic change—the kind of change that deeply transforms your life and your greater world—comes from that deep, heartfelt, empowering hunger and an unstoppable desire to do something BIG, like GALACTIC BIG, and purposeful. So make that desire a juicy one, Shiny! Make it so BIG, so bright and so Shiny that sets your heart on fire if you know what I am talking about, my dear! Set your cosmic heart on fire!!! This is how you do it! This is how you bring forth the best in U! This is how you change your own galactic orbit from boring brown to hot pink, my darling Shiny. ⭐ And this is how you SHINE! Be bold and brave, my star-shine! Be diamond sharp! Simply, be galactic!

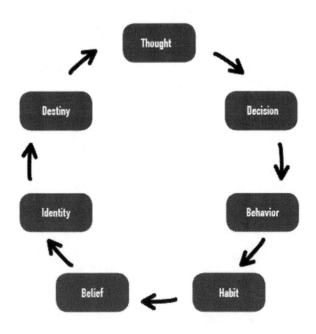

You see, Shiny, life will keep happening, things will keep changing and people will keep being and doing what they know, regardless if you like it or not. The rain will rain again, the sun will move again and, yes, your cosmic power will shine again! ☆ If only you choose to see that the universe has its laws, my darling, showing you the way, guiding you to the light in times of darkness. Had we not covered the Cosmic Law of Polarity that you can only shine in the dark? Look at the stars in the sky, my lovely lady. Look and see how things are upstairs! Because by showing you how it's done upstairs, the universe, our Shiny creator of all the things, beings and feelings, is calling out the Leader in U, simply to take care of your things downstairs.

And by now, you already know the hierarchy of the universe, darling. You know that applying the very obvious secret laws of our universe in the order it was received is what it takes to be a galactic eeing! Because that's what a galactic leader does: She shines!

A galactic leader knows how to ask to receive.

She knows what to Be-Live because she also knows that her system is going to do whatever it takes to make her right about what she Be-Lives, so she artfully and carefully chooses what to Be-Live!

She knows that how she does one thing is how she does everything. So she artfully and cosmically measures her behaviors first, and then she generates new, Shiny and galactic behaviors that are not only elevating her soul but also pushing all the beings forward!

She also knows that the best view is seen from the top. So she knows where to go in times of troubles and darkness: Above! She artfully and easily reminds herself that she is stardust, a part of this divine order, in need of unity and oneness. Then she can see again the cosmic hands in everything and re-sets her galactic vision in her life.

A galactic leader also knows that wherever her mind goes, her energy flows. So she powerfully and elegantly directs her thoughts throughout her day. She is a master in managing her focus and, eventually, her moods. And that's simply why she is able to generate her own electrified cosmic energy!

When a galactic leader is in the flow, she knows that she will glow! And since she knows that very well, she also implements it very well. She knows what her flow is and she puts herself in that flow over and over and over again. Because that's where she would like to live. ⭐ In the flow of her Shiny galactic being. ⭐

A galactic leader is and can only be a galactic leader when another galactic leader recognizes her shining galactic power! And for this reason, a galactic leader only hangs out with other galactic leaders. Because she knows that who you hang out with is who you eventually become in your galactic path!

As for resources, regardless of having the resources or not, a galactic leader knows how to be resourceful and create her own alternative ways to get things done! Because in the end, it's really not the resources that make the biggest change in life, it is your resourcefulness. ⭐

A galactic leader is a critical, creative and practical thinker. So she knows that doing the same thing over and over again and expecting different results is insanity. As the strategic thinker that she is, she is able to integrate both the art and the science of shining bright like a galactic diamond. ⭐

Because she knows that the queen of all her Shiny skills is repetition, repetition and repetition, my dear. ⭐ By repetition you'll be doing your muscle-creation! ENJOY! **Ms. Sparkle!** ⭐

> ## Return on Action: NEURO-SHINE™ (Neuro-muscle creation)

My dearest Shiny, here you are at your heightened consciousness as a super bright galactic leader. Here you are at a new beginning to live your cosmic life. Here you are with advanced life technologies to integrate what you see upstairs with what you live downstairs. Here you are as your newest version wrapped up in a gift box from the universe. Filled with wisdom, filled with love, filled with life again. Here you are at a point of decision to either lead a life of desperation or a Shiny and happy life of inspiration. Here you are at the moment of your creative expression. A moment of creation, expression and also celebration.

CREATION of the new U, your higher self as called out from the universe. Creation of the new U, your shiniest and happiest vibration as a leader of your life! Creation of the new U, as your ultimate version with all that U are as a galactic leader, not only as a leader of your life but also as a leader of many other cosmic lives! Leading, guiding and shining so many other galaxies for so many other galactic leaders to breakthrough their physical and transit fears so as to enjoy and celebrate their galactic beings! So as to BE U!

EXPRESSION of the new life in every inch of your physical body, each and every single cell of your brain as the most present, the most joyous and the most enthusiastic life you can possibly live. Expression of the new life charged up with your freedom, your creativity, your intelligence and your own identity. Expression of your meaning and your purpose in life, in every single thing you do, with your heart smiling every moment. 🌟 So as to LIVE U!

And the CELEBRATION of your time, your "NOW" with your new Shiny and happy beliefs in it, your reasons WHY, your talents, your skills, your rules, your terms and more U in your moments. So as to BELIEVE IN U. Since you know, it is the only way for a Galactic Leader like you, to BE "LIVE" IN U!

So now, just put a cosmic smile on your face, BE the newest version of YOU and let the **NEURO-SHINE™** activity help you to recreate that SHINY & HAPPY U, darling!

And remember, after all these cosmic wing steps you have taken, you are now going to HAVE all the SHINY & HAPPY feelings you have been longing to HAVE along your galactic path, my dear stardust. Because now you know it's not the physical or material things that you really want to HAVE, it is these incredible vibration of BEING feelings you want to FEEL, through this COSMIC BEING you have **already** BEcome, my inter-galactic, cosmic star friend! ⭐ **Welcome home...**

Neuro-Shine™

NEURO-SHINE™

Imagine You are the Brightest Star Dancing Shiny & Happy in the Sky; and start moving & dancing

Self-talk about Your Shiny & Happy Moments with Your Shiny Happy Self

Feel your neurons' shine in your smile!

Start saying that you are a Shiny and Happy Star with a rhythm: Sing Your Shiny Song

Pick Your Shiny Music & Start Listening and Enjoying Your Shiny Self with Upbeats

Focus on All Your Shiny and Happy Moments when Dancing

Shiny Burcu Unsal

Do's and Don'ts for a Galactic Leader

Here is a list of what to do and what not to do as a Galactic Leader. These tips are great reminders for you to Be-Live in U even during not that yummy times my wonderful space queen ;)

With these everyday intergalactic "identity reminders", on top of all the steps you have taken so far, it is now official that you have become an unstoppable GALACTIC LEADER! ☆ Congratulations! ☆

Now that you remembered who you really were in your core as a magnificent, powerful cosmic SUPERSTAR and you were actually born to SHINE, what are you waiting for my darling? Go ahead and own it! Make some soul-felt decisions and take some intergalactic actions! Go get your life back superstar! You know you can do it! 'Cos it's your time to shine!

XOXO, The Shiny One ☆

DO's for a GALACTIC LEADER	DON'Ts for a GALACTIC LEADER
Be present	Don't live in the past or in the future
Love yourself & your life	Don't talk negative about yourself
Remember your time is limited here	Don't take things for granted in life
Put yourself first in everything you do	Don't do things just because others wanted
Have a positive attitude in life	Don't complain or blame others
Make sure you enjoy every moment in life	Don't let your time pass empty
Be curious about life, about people	Don't judge people without asking questions
Have an open mind to learn from everyone	Don't operate with "I know it all" attitude
Know WHO you want to Be	Don't be an unconscious, unaware being
Remember to smile all the time! ☆	Don't cheat the world of your smile ☆
Add a little fun in everything	Don't be boring
Find resources to feel good ☆	Don't be stuck with problems
Have your own rituals with yourself	Don't live an automatic, robotic life
Be kind, polite and elegant	Don't be rude, disrespectful or classless
Know your WHY, your mission in life	Don't just do things randomly
Commit to your higher purpose	Don't give up on your life, your purpose
Be bold and brave in life	Don't be scared of taking risks
Be larger than your life	Don't think small
Learn critical thinking skills	Don't be dumb!
Be resourceful and creative for your life	Don't act like you don't have a brain
Be aware of your excuses and limiting beliefs	Don't let your FEAR take over control
Always look for ways to grow	Don't stop learning, reading, training, etc.
Listen to learn	Don't listen to talk back!
Have your own rules and standards in life	Don't say yes to everything and no to nothing

DO's for a GALACTIC LEADER	DON'Ts for a GALACTIC LEADER
Teach others how to treat you	Don't assume people know what you want
Be understanding for others' life conditions	Don't be cruel, you don't know their story
Be the LEADER of your life	Don't act like a child with no responsibilities
Set yourself motivating goals	Don't forget your higher purpose
Be laser-focused on your goals	Don't get distracted
Measure your goals regularly	Don't just set goals and forget about them
Generate energy when you need it	Don't complain that you have no energy
Compliment & praise others generously	Don't be sarcastic and criticizing
Learn how to communicate better	Don't be annoying, don't argue or get angry
Contribute to the world	Don't sit at home and do nothing!
Give your 100% in everything you do	Don't do it just to finish it
Choose empowering language	Don't talk negative
Be a lady of your word with integrity	Don't give up on your words and promises
Be happy and shiny ☆	Don't let others stop you
Use NLP Techniques	Don't feel overwhelmed
Be an inspiration for others	Don't be a desperation for others
Use your Contextual Intelligence	Don't generalize everything in life
Be a visionary leader	Don't think in a box
Live your life in your own terms	Don't just take what's given; get what U want
Be loving and caring	Don't forget that people need love and care
Set an example of a good human being	Don't forget to inspire
Live your life in your own terms	Don't settle with anything less than U deserve

Acknowledgements

God bless your Shiny soul my dear father, my inspiration, **Esat Unsal**. You gave me my first wings to fly and speak. Without you, I couldn't be who I am today, The Shiny One. I love you.

Thank you my sweet mommy, **Gunsel Unsal**. ☆ For pushing me to become a better version of me all my life…. My first teacher, my shoulder to cry on, my idol to carry on. You deserve the brightest galaxies in your heart. ☆ Without you, I wouldn't be who I am today, The Shiny One. ☆ I love you.

Thank you, my dear brother, **Ali Cem Unsal,** for introducing me to the world of NLP in 2003. Without you, I wouldn't be who I am today, The Shiny One. ☆ I love you.

Thank you, **Mr. Cahit Ceylan** for letting me taste what advertising is.

Thank you, **Mrs. Eren Irdiren**, for letting me start my career in the advertising industry.

God bless your soul, my one and only **Anooshjun, Anoosh Saei.** Without you, I wouldn't be who I am today, The Shiny One. ☆

Thank you, **Mr. Joe Phelps**, for believing in me and literally reshaping my perspective about life, about people and about my career. I owe you my greatest gratitudes.

Thank you so much, Mr. **Firuz Baglikaya,** for believing in me and making me rise above my fears.

Thank you, Mr. **Murat Serim,** for waking me up to my strengths and my power within!

Thank you, dear **Volkan Keskinoglu**, for coming into my life and creating a miraculous opportunity for me to grow more and define the new me.

Thank you, **Dr. Richard Bandler**, our universe is a shinier place because of your genius! If you did not come up with NLP, our planet would NEVER be as SHINY & HAPPY like this today!

Thank you, **Anthony Robbins**, our galaxy is a better place because you exist in it!

Thank you, Mr. **Van Anderson**, for letting me share my light with the best students in the world at UCLA Extension.

Thank you, Mr. **Caglar Coroglu**, for making me an official motivational speaker at your stages.

Thank you, **Ozgur Atanur**, for seeing my light and opening your loving heart for me for this book. Without you, I don't know when I would finish this book. ⭐

Thank you, **Adam Markel**, for being who you are, a fantastic, glamourous nebula! Our galaxy needs more galactic leaders like you! You touched my heart so deep with your heart and you moved my soul so high with your cosmic being that you literally make the Shiny one shine!

Thank you, dear **Veronica Tan and Richard Tan**, for being my true friends and helping me become better and dream bigger every single day! Keep transforming our planet leaders!

Thank you, **Chris Kay**, for Be-Live'ing in me! You are a living example of a true galactic leader! I cherish the day I met you, Mr. Awesome, the HOW GUY, who teaches others to take their life to the next level! ☆

Thank you, **Tony Materna**, for being my mentor, my super intelligent, rocket-scientist friend, and my source of wisdom to go to. I highly appreciate your existence in my life!

Thank you, **Brendon Burchard** and **Marie Forleo**, for being my biggest inspirations to keep going everyday for my dream! Both of you are amazing galactic leaders for our planet!

And thank you, my lovely **COSMIC LIFE**, for giving me a second chance to prove who I really am inside! That I really am a shining light for so many. I LOVE YOU, too! ☆

So let there be light and let it shine bright! ☆

XOXO, The Shiny One

Shiny Burcu Unsal, assisting Dr. Richard Bandler
in Orlando/FL in 2015

Shiny Burcu Unsal, with Tony Robbins at
Business Mastery in London in 2016

Shiny Burcu Unsal with Brendon Burchard
at WGST in Santa Clara/CA in 2016

Shiny Burcu Unsal, in her Shiny Happy NLP
Transformation Event in Los Angeles in 2016

Shiny Burcu Unsal, in her Online NLP Training in 2015

Shiny Burcu Unsal, in her Online NLP Training in 2015

Shiny Burcu Unsal, in her Online NLP Training in 2015

Shiny Burcu Unsal, at Marketing Conference in 2015

Shiny Burcu Unsal, at Leadership Conference in 2014

https://www.facebook.com/ShinyUnsal

Instagram: https://www.instagram.com/shinyunsal/

Website: www.Be-LiveinU.com
        www.TheShinyOne.com
        www.shinyhappynlp.com

Linkedin: www.linkedin.com/in/ShinyUnsal

YouTube: https://www.youtube.com/c/beliveinutv

Online Courses:
http://www.be-liveinu-training.com/

Printed in the United States
By Bookmasters